Final Accounts Preparation

Tutorial

David Cox

Published by Osborne Books Limited
Tel 01905 748071
Email books@osbornebooks.co.uk
Website www.osbornebooks.co.uk

Design by Laura Ingham

Printed by CPI Group (UK) Limited, Croydon, CR0 4YY, on environmentally friendly, acid-free paper from managed forests.

MIX
Paper from
responsible sources
FSC® C019777
FSC
www.fsc.org

British Library Cataloguing in Publication Data
A catalogue record for this book is available from the British Library

ISBN 978 1909173 798

Contents

Also available from Osborne Books...

Workbooks

Practice questions and assessments
with answers

Wise Guides

Handy pocket-sized study and revision guides

Student Zone

Login to access your free ebooks and
interactive revision crosswords

Introduction

Qualifications covered

This book has been written specifically to cover the Unit 'Final Accounts Preparation' which is mandatory for the following qualifications:

AAT Advanced Diploma in Accounting – Level 3

AAT Advanced Certificate in Bookkeeping – Level 3

AAT Advanced Diploma in Accounting at SCQF – Level 6

Further Education and Training Certificate: Accounting Technician – (Level 4 AATSA)

The book contains a clear text with worked examples and case studies, chapter summaries and key terms to help with revision. Each chapter concludes with a wide range of activities, many in the style of AAT computer based assessments.

Osborne Study and Revision Materials

The materials featured on the previous page are tailored to the needs of students studying this unit and revising for the assessment. They include:

- **Workbooks:** paperback books with practice activities and exams
- **Wise Guides:** pocket-sized spiral bound revision cards
- **Student Zone:** access to Osborne Books online resources
- **Osborne Books App:** Osborne Books ebooks for mobiles and tablets

Visit www.osbornebooks.co.uk for details of study and revision resources and access to online material.

1 Business organisations

this chapter covers...

In this chapter we take an overview of business organisations, including the financial recording and reporting requirements of each.

We begin by looking at the various organisations, including a brief description, differences between them, and the financial characteristics of each.

The terminology used is explained – including the terms used to represent ownership or net assets.

The regulations – legislation, accounting standards, statements of recommended practice – are considered.

The role of accounting staff in the financial recording and reporting requirements of each organisation is considered, including the importance of deadlines in the preparation of their financial statements.

DIFFERENT TYPES OF BUSINESS ORGANISATIONS

Accounting staff will be involved in the financial recording and reporting requirements of a number of types of business organisations. Some businesses will be concerned with reporting the profit or loss that they have made for the accounting period, while others will be concerned with the amount and availability of their net assets.

In this chapter we can distinguish between businesses that are:

- for profit: sole trader, partnership, limited liability partnership, and limited company
- not-for-profit: charity

The diagram on page 4 shows the main differences between the structure and financial characteristics of each. Firstly though, the table which follows gives a brief description of each type of organisation.

For Profit	
sole trader	an individual in business, trading in his or her name, or under a trading name
partnership	a group of individuals working together as partners in business
limited liability partnership (LLP)	an incorporated* form of partnership, with a separate legal entity, where members are able to limit their personal liability for the debts of the business
limited company	an incorporated* business, with a separate legal entity, owned by shareholders and run by directors
Not-for-Profit	
charity	an organisation, run by trustees, which uses its resources to fund charitable activities under its control

*incorporated = formed into a legal corporation, ie a separate legal body

Structure and Financial Characteristics of Business and Charity Organisations

	Sole Trader	Partnership	Limited Liability Partnership (LLP)	Limited Company	Charity
Ownership	sole trader owns the business	the partners own the business	owned by members but a separate legal entity	owned by shareholders but a separate legal entity	run by trustees for charitable purposes for the public benefit
Management	sole trader manages the business	all partners entitled to take an active role	all members entitled to take an active role	run by directors on behalf of shareholders	trustees run the charity
Responsibility for debts	owner is liable for entire debt of business	partners are each liable for entire debt of partnership	members can lose up to their investment in the LLP	shareholders can lose up to their investment in the company	for unincorporated charities (ie not formed as a company) trustees may be liable for debts of the charity
Taxation of profits	income tax on profits paid by the owner	each partner liable for income tax on their share of profits	each member liable for income tax on their share of profits	corporation tax paid on the profits of the company	exempt from tax when income used for charitable purposes
Ownership terminology	capital	capital	capital	equity	net assets form the funds of the charity
Distributions	drawings by owner	drawings by partners	drawings by members	dividends paid to shareholders	distributions for charitable activities
Accounting regulations	• none • financial statements are private and not available to public	• Partnership Act, 1890 • partnership agreement • financial statements are private and not available to public	• Limited Liability Partnership Act, 2000 • LLP agreement • financial statements are available to the public through Companies House	• Companies Act, 2006 • Financial Reporting Standards • financial statements are available to the public through Companies House	• Charities Act, 2011 • Charity regulators – the Charity Commission • Statement of Recommended Practice (SORP) or FRS (Financial Reporting Standard) 102 • financial statements are available to the public through the Charity Commission

SOLE TRADERS

Sole traders are people who run their own businesses, for example shops, factories, farms, garages, local franchises - they are also referred to as 'self-employed'. The businesses are generally small because the owner usually has a limited amount of capital. Profits are often small and, after the owner has taken out drawings, are usually ploughed back into the business.

advantages and disadvantages

Sole trader businesses are cheap and easy to set up; the **advantages** are:

- the owner has independence and can run the business, often without the need to consult others
- after payment of business expenses, all profits belong to the owner
- in a small business with few, if any, employees, personal service and supervision by the owner are available at all times
- the business is easy to establish legally – either using the owner's name, or a trading name such as 'The Fashion Shop' or 'Wyvern Plumbers'

The **disadvantages** are:

- the owner has unlimited liability for the debts of the business – this means that if the sole trader should become insolvent, the owner's personal assets may be used to pay business debts
- all losses of the business are the owner's responsibility
- expansion is limited because it can only be achieved by the owner ploughing back profits, or by borrowing from a lender such as a bank
- the owner usually has to work long hours and it may be difficult to find time to take holidays; if the owner should become ill the work of the business will either slow down or stop altogether

financial statements of a sole trader

The financial statements (final accounts) of a sole trader comprise:

- statement of profit or loss
- statement of financial position

Such financial statements are produced annually at the end of the financial year (which can end at any date – it doesn't have to be the calendar year). The financial statements can be produced more often in order to give information to the sole trader on how the business is progressing.

For sole trader financial statements:

- there is no definitive format
- there is no specific legislation
- there are no accounting rules in the form of accounting standards
- there are no annual returns to make to Companies House

The sole trader is responsible to HM Revenue & Customs:

- for annual income tax returns, stating the profit of the business
- for Value Added Tax, if the business is registered for VAT, making quarterly or annual returns and payments (or receiving repayments)

The accounting rules of sole trader businesses and the preparation of their financial statements are set out in detail in Chapter 5.

PARTNERSHIPS

Normally, partnerships consist of between two and twenty partners (exceptions being large, professional businesses, eg solicitors and accountants). Partnerships are often larger businesses than sole traders because, as there is more than one owner, there is likely to be more capital. A partnership may be formed to set up a new business or it may be the logical growth of a sole trader taking in partners to increase the capital.

The rules of the partnership are set out either in the Partnership Act 1890 or in a Partnership Agreement (which may be written or oral) made between the partners.

advantages and disadvantages

Partnerships are cheap and easy to set up; the **advantages** over a sole trader business are:

- there is the possibility of increased capital
- individual partners may be able to specialise in particular areas of the business
- with more people running the business, there is cover for illness and holidays

The **disadvantages** over a sole trader business are:

- as there is more than one owner, decisions may take longer because other partners may need to be consulted
- there may be disagreements amongst the partners

■ each partner is liable in law for the dealings and business debts of the **whole** business (unless it is a 'limited liability partnership' – see next section)

■ the retirement or death of one partner may adversely affect the running of the business

financial statements of a partnership

A partnership prepares the same type of financial statements (final accounts) as a sole trader:

■ statement of profit or loss

■ statement of financial position

The financial statements show how the profit from the statement of profit or loss is shared out amongst the partners, and incorporate the accounting rules either of the Partnership Act 1890 or of the Partnership Agreement made between the partners.

For partnership financial statements:

■ there is no definitive format

■ there is no specific legislation (although the Partnership Act 1890 may apply regarding sharing of profits or losses)

■ there are no accounting rules in the form of accounting standards

■ there are no annual returns to make to Companies House

The partnership is responsible to HM Revenue & Customs for Value Added Tax, if the business is registered for VAT, making quarterly or annual returns and payments (or receiving repayments). Each partner is responsible to HM Revenue & Customs for his or her annual income tax return, stating their share of the profit of the partnership.

The accounting rules of partnership businesses and the preparation of their financial statements are set out in detail in Chapter 6.

INCORPORATED STATUS

A company or other organisation is incorporated by being formed into a legal corporation separate from its owners. There are two main types of businesses with incorporated status:

■ limited liability partnerships (LLPs)

■ limited companies

advantages of incorporation

■ the main advantage of incorporation is, without doubt, the limit on the liability for members (LLP) and shareholders (limited company) to the amount of their investment

Other advantages include:

■ the continuing existence of the business as a separate legal entity

■ an enhancement of the credibility of the business, eg a limited company sounds a more substantial business than a sole trader

■ access to finance may be easier

■ transfer of ownership of the business may be easier, eg the sale of shares in a limited company

disadvantages of incorporation

■ the main disadvantage is the more complex requirements of setting up the business and then the higher costs of keeping up with record keeping and annual returns

Other disadvantages include:

■ information filed with Companies House is in the public domain so anyone can access financial and other details

■ business finances must be kept entirely separate from those of the owners, which contrasts with a sole trader who can take drawings from the business as and when required

limited liability partnerships

An LLP is often the preferred business format for professional partnerships, such as accountants and solicitors, because of the limited liability protection. Other businesses might choose to be LLPs instead of forming limited companies.

An LLP is set up through a process of legal incorporation, which requires certain documents to be submitted to the Registrar of Companies at Companies House. It is also advisable – but not a legal requirement – for an LLP to have a Members' Agreement setting out the rights, duties and obligations of members – this may be written or oral. (Note that although an LLP is a partnership, those owning the business are called 'members' and not 'partners'.) All LLPs must have two or more 'designated members' who are responsible for ensuring that the legal and accounting requirements are carried out, eg keeping accounting records, arranging for the accounts to be audited if required, preparing and submitting the LLP's Annual Return to Companies House, etc.

The financial statements (final accounts) of an LLP, which form part of the Annual Return, are very similar to those of limited companies – see below – and comprise:

- statement of profit or loss
- statement of financial position
- supporting notes to the financial statements (the depth of information required varies with the size of the LLP)
- Auditor's Report (smaller LLPs may be exempt from audit)

The financial statements show how the profit from the statement of profit or loss is shared out amongst the members and incorporates the accounting rules of the Members' Agreement.

The accounting requirements, including the level of detail to be disclosed together with the order of items in the statements of profit or loss and financial position, are set out in FRS 102: The Financial Reporting Standard applicable in the UK and Republic of Ireland. Sample layouts of financial statements are given in FRS 102.

The Annual Return must be filed at Companies House, by the designated members of the LLP, where it is available for public inspection.

limited companies

Limited companies incorporate by registering under the Companies Act 2006 and by submitting certain documents to the Registrar of Companies at Companies House. The Articles of Association set out the written rules about running the company that have been agreed by the shareholders, directors, and the company secretary (model Articles of Association are available from the Companies House at www.gov.uk).

Once registered, a company is run by the directors on behalf of the shareholders. It is a responsibility of the directors to submit the company's Annual Return to Companies House. The financial statements, which form part of the Annual Return, comprise:

- statement of profit or loss
- statement of financial position
- supporting notes to the financial statements (the depth of information required varies with the size of the company)
- directors' report to shareholders
- Auditor's Report (smaller limited companies may be exempt from audit)

Companies follow the accounting rules set out in the Companies Act 2006 and in Financial Reporting Standards (or International Financial Reporting Standards). Sample layouts of the statement of profit or loss and financial position are provided within these, including the level of detail to be disclosed, together with the order in which items are to be stated.

The company's Annual Return must be filed at Companies House, by the directors, where it is available for public inspection.

Chapter 8 gives more detail of the financial statements of limited companies.

CHARITIES

Charities are set up to provide charitable activities within the scope of the charity. Most of their income is from donations, grants and funding; most of their expenditure is finance for their charitable activities.

The main rules governing charities are set out in:

- the Charities Act 2011
- the Charity Commission, which is the regulator for most charities
- the Statement of Recommended Practice (SORP) Accounting and Reporting by charities, or FRS 102, *The Financial Reporting Standard applicable in the UK and Ireland*

Charities are restricted in what they can do and how they work:

- they must follow charity law

- their purpose must be for public benefit
- they are governed by a trust deed, which sets out the name of the charity, its objects and powers, and deals with the appointment of trustees, how meetings are to be run, and the required financial statements (a model Trust Deed is available from the Charity Commission at www.gov.uk)
- they are run by trustees, who do not usually benefit personally from the charity but, under certain circumstances, could become liable for the debts of the charity
- they are independent of other organisations
- most charities must register with the Charity Commission

All but the smallest charities prepare financial statements which comprise:

- statement of financial activities
- statement of financial position
- cashflow statement (required for certain charities)

- supporting notes to the financial statements
- trustees' Annual Report (which must be available on request by interested parties)
- Auditor's Report (large charities) or Independent Examiner's Report (medium-sized charities), but no audit is normally required for small charities

These comprise the charity's Annual Return which must be filed by the trustees with the Charity Commission where it is available for public inspection.

THE ROLE OF THE ACCOUNTANT

Each of the business organisations and charitable organisations that we have studied in this chapter will require the involvement of accounting staff. This involvement will range from recording day-to-day accounting transactions, through preparing the annual financial statements and, where required, conducting a year end audit and reporting to interested parties that financial transactions have been dealt with correctly.

Whatever work they undertake – whether paid for or not (many charities look for accounting staff to help them on a voluntary basis) – it must be carried out:

- professionally
- in a competent manner
- with due care

These mean that accounting staff should maintain their professional knowledge and skill at the level required to ensure that an employer or client receives a competent service. They should act diligently in accordance with current developments in practice, legislation and techniques. They should ensure that their behaviour complies with relevant laws and regulations and avoids bringing the accountancy profession into disrepute.

Of great importance for all organisations is to ensure that deadlines are met in the preparation and submission of financial statements. This could be the completion of year end financial statements to enable sole traders and partnerships to complete their tax returns to HM Revenue & Customs, the filing of the Annual Return of limited liability partnerships and limited companies with Companies House, or the filing of a charity's financial statements and trustees' Annual Report with the Charity Commission.

Chapter Summary	▧ Accounting staff will be involved with the financial recording and reporting requirements of a number of types of business organisations.
	▧ For profit organisations: sole trader, partnership, limited liability partnership, and limited company.
	▧ Not for profit organisations: charity.
	▧ In the statement of financial position of for profit organisations, ownership is capital or equity, and amounts taken by, or paid to, the owner(s) is drawings or dividends.
	▧ In the statement of financial position of not for profit organisations, net assets form the funds of the charity, and distributions are made for charitable activities.
	▧ Sole trader and partnership businesses are cheap and easy to form, but self-employed individuals are fully liable for the entire debt of the business.
	▧ Limited liability partnerships and limited companies are more complex to form, but provide limited liability to members and shareholders for their investment in the business.
	▧ Sole trader businesses often have less scope for expansion when compared with partnerships which may have increased capital and partners who are able to specialise in particular areas of the business.
	▧ When preparing the financial statements of businesses and charities, accounting staff must carry out their work professionally, in a competent manner, and act with due care.
	▧ It is important for all organisations to meet the required deadlines for the preparation of their financial statements.

Key Terms	**sole trader**	an individual in business
	partnership	a group of individuals working together as partners in business
	incorporated	a business formed into a legal corporation
	limited liability partnership (LLP)	an incorporated form of partnership, with a separate legal entity, where members are able to limit their personal liability for the debts of the business
	limited company	an incorporated business, with a separate legal entity, owned by shareholders and run by directors
	charity	an organisation, run by trustees, which uses its resources to fund charitable activities under its control

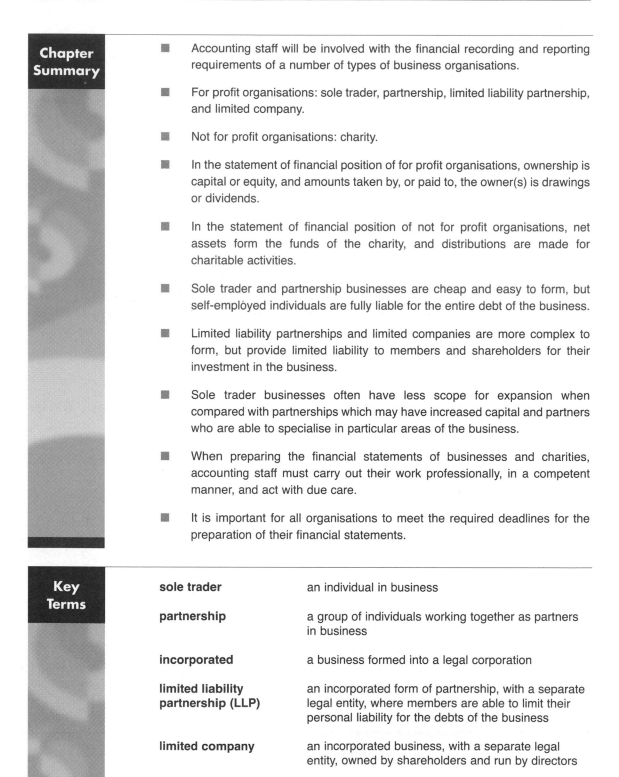

Activities

1.1 A friend of yours, Zara, is keen to set up in business running a sandwich and coffee shop on her own. Note down some points for a discussion with her, listing the advantages and disadvantages of a sole trader business, and possible future developments in the business organisation that she might consider.

1.2 **(a)** Define a partnership.

(b) Explain how a limited liability partnership differs from an ordinary partnership.

1.3 Office Systems Limited wishes to prepare an information sheet for new staff explaining some facts about limited companies.

You are to prepare the information sheet which explains:

(a) who owns Office Systems Limited?

(b) who is responsible for the day-to-day running of Office Systems Limited?

(c) what is the meaning of limited liability?

1.4 **(a)** Explain what is meant by incorporation.

(b) Give two advantages and two disadvantages of incorporation.

1.5 **(a)** Define a charity.

(b) What are the main rules that govern charities?

1.6 Investigate the financial structure of an organisation – either for profit or not for profit – with which you are familiar. In particular, identify:

(a) who owns the organisation, or the public benefit requirement?

(b) who manages the organisation?

(c) where responsibility for debts lies if the organisation cannot pay, and note any limits of liability.

(d) whether, and how, any tax is paid.

2 Framework of accounting

this chapter covers...

The focus of this chapter is the users of financial statements, and the framework within which accountants work. The chapter covers:

■ *the primary users of financial statements, and why they are needed by these users*

■ *the framework of accounting, which comprises accounting principles, accounting policies and characteristics, and ethical principles*

■ *the application of ethical principles when preparing financial statements*

USERS OF FINANCIAL STATEMENTS

The main – or primary – users of financial statements include:

- owner(s)/existing and potential investors
- lenders, eg banks
- suppliers
- employees
- customers
- government agencies, eg HM Revenue & Customs, Charity Commission
- the public

The diagram which follows shows in detail the primary users and why the financial statements are needed by these users.

Primary users of financial statements

User of financial statements	Why the financial statements are needed
Owner(s)/existing and potential investors	• To see how much profit has been made • To see how much money can be paid out in drawings/dividends • To see the net asset value of the business and whether it has increased or decreased • To assess if the business will continue in the foreseeable future
Lenders, eg banks	• To see how much profit has been made • To check that the business will be able to pay interest on loans and make loan repayments • To assess how much of the business is being funded by the lender • To see what security is available to cover loans
Suppliers	• To decide whether to supply goods and services to the business • To assess if the business is able to pay its suppliers
Employees	• To assess whether the business is able to pay wages and salaries • To consider whether the business will continue to offer employment in the future
Customers	• To see if the business will be able to continue supplying its goods and services • To assess the ability of the business to provide service in the future, eg spare parts, and to meet warranty liabilities
Government agencies eg HM Revenue & Customs, Charity Commission	• To ensure that, if appropriate, the business is registered for VAT • To calculate the tax due – either income tax for sole traders and partnerships or corporation tax for limited companies • To ensure that the charity is being run correctly
The public	• To assess the contribution to the economy • To assess employment prospects

It should be noted, however, that not all users will have access to the financial statements of all types of business. As noted in the previous chapter, the statements of sole traders and partnerships are not generally in the public domain – although a bank lending money to a business will expect to see them. For businesses that file an annual return with Companies House – ie limited liability partnerships and limited companies – information is in the public domain. Likewise, charities file an annual report to the Charity Commission where it is available for public inspection.

WHAT IS MEANT BY THE FRAMEWORK OF ACCOUNTING?

The framework of accounting sets out the conventions that underlie the financial recording and reporting of business accounts. Accounting staff work within this framework in the preparation of financial statements.

The framework consists of three main areas:

■ accounting principles

■ accounting policies and characteristics

■ ethical principles of accounting

These are summarised in the diagram below.

FRAMEWORK OF ACCOUNTING	
Accounting principles	• business entity • materiality • going concern basis • accrual basis
Accounting policies and characteristics	• application of accounting policies • fundamental qualitative characteristics • supporting qualitative characteristics
Ethical principles	• integrity • objectivity • professional competence and due care • confidentiality • professional behaviour

UNDERLYING ASSUMPTIONS OF ACCOUNTING PRINCIPLES

Accounting principles (or concepts) underlie the financial recording and reporting requirements of different types of organisations. Accounting principles help to ensure that the records and statements prepared are relevant and reliable to users, and that they are comparable and understandable. In particular, accounting principles help to ensure that financial records and statements are fit to be used for:

- **internal control** – within the business to ensure that the financial records are accurate and that the financial statements show the true position of the business

- **measuring business performance** – both internally and externally – so that financial reports and statements can be compared

- **obtaining credit/financing** – providing lenders with the current financial position of the business

- **statutory requirements** – providing information for tax and other purposes when required to do so by law

The diagram below illustrates the important accounting principles – we will look in more detail at these principles over the next few pages

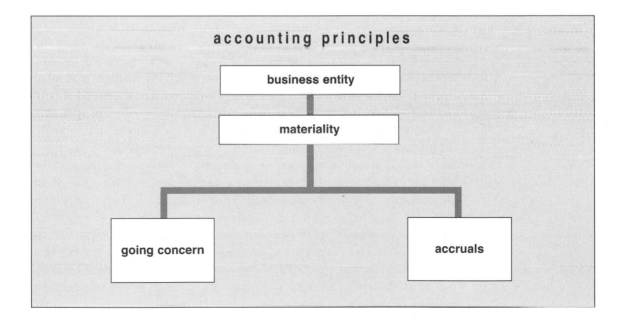

business entity

This refers to the fact that financial statements record and report on the activities of one particular business or organisation. They do not include the assets and liabilities of those who play a part in owning or running the business. Thus the personal assets and liabilities of the owner/owners are kept separate from those of the business: the main links between the business and the personal funds of the owner/owners are capital and drawings.

materiality

Some items in accounts are of such low value that it is not worthwhile recording them separately, ie they are not 'material'. For example, small items, such as donations to charities, the purchase of plants for the office, window cleaning, etc, may be grouped together in a sundry expenses account. Low cost non-current assets, such as a stapler or a waste bin, are treated as an expense rather than capital expenditure.

Materiality depends very much on the size of the business. For example, a large company may consider that the cost of items of less than £1,000 are not material; by contrast, a small business may use a much lower amount, perhaps £100. It is for a business to set a policy as to what amount is material and what is not.

Note that materiality is considered to be part of the fundamental qualitative characteristic of **relevance** – see next page.

going concern

Going concern presumes that the business to which the financial statements relate will continue to trade in the foreseeable future. The statement of profit or loss and statement of financial position are prepared on the basis that there is no intention to significantly reduce the size of the business or to liquidate the business. Note that, if a business is no longer a going concern, assets will have very different values, and the statement of financial position will be affected considerably. For example, a large, purpose-built factory has considerable value to a going concern business but, if the factory had to be sold, it is likely to have a limited use for other industries, and therefore will have a lower market value. Values based on liquidation amounts are the opposite of the going concern and require extra depreciation to be charged as an expense to the statement of profit or loss to allow for the reduced value of non-current assets. In a similar way, inventory that is to be sold in a clearance sale will be reduced in value.

accruals

This means that income and expenses are matched so that they relate to the same goods or services and the same accounting period. This means that the statement of profit or loss shows the amount of the expense incurred, and the amount of income earned, rather than reflecting payments and receipts when they happened. Examples of the use of accruals in accounting are:

- accruals
- prepayments
- provision for depreciation charges
- allowance for doubtful debts
- cost of inventory

ACCOUNTING POLICIES AND CHARACTERISTICS

Accounting policies are the methods used by a business to show the effect of financial transactions, and to record assets and liabilities in the statement of financial position. For example, a business may choose as its accounting policy to depreciate its office equipment, using the straight-line method, at 25 per cent per year.

In order for financial information to be useful, a business selects its accounting policies to fit in with the two fundamental qualitative accounting characteristics of:

- *relevance* – financial information that is useful to users of the financial statements (note that for information to be relevant, it must also be material – see the accounting principle of materiality on the previous page)
- *faithful representation* – financial information must correspond to the effect of transactions or events, and, as far as possible, should be complete, neutral, and free from error

The following four accounting characteristics support relevance and faithful representation:

- *comparability* – financial statements can be compared with those from previous years and with similar businesses
- *verifiability* – users of financial statements are assured that the information given is faithfully represented, eg inventory valuations
- *timeliness* – users of financial statements receive information in time to enable decisions to be made
- *understandability* – financial information is presented clearly and concisely so that users can understand the information given

The characteristics of useful financial information are shown in the following diagram.

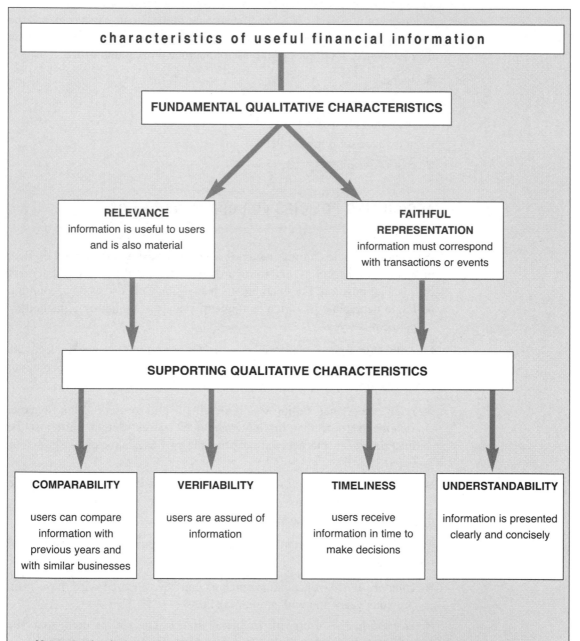

characteristics of useful financial information

FUNDAMENTAL QUALITATIVE CHARACTERISTICS

RELEVANCE
information is useful to users and is also material

FAITHFUL REPRESENTATION
information must correspond with transactions or events

SUPPORTING QUALITATIVE CHARACTERISTICS

COMPARABILITY

users can compare information with previous years and with similar businesses

VERIFIABILITY

users are assured of information

TIMELINESS

users receive information in time to make decisions

UNDERSTANDABILITY

information is presented clearly and concisely

Note: the fundamental qualitative characteristics and the supporting qualitative characteristics are taken from the International Financial Reporting Standards *Framework for Financial Reporting* document, which sets out the principles that underlie the preparation and presentation of financial statements.

MATERIAL MISSTATEMENT

We have seen earlier in this chapter who are the primary users of financial statements. The users rely on the accuracy of financial statements to make economic decisions – eg to invest in the business, to lend money to the business, to supply goods and services to the business. It is important that, when preparing financial statements, accounting staff should ensure that such statements are free from 'material misstatement'.

Material misstatement can be defined as 'when information contained in the financial statements is untrue - whether accidentally or intentionally – and could influence the economic decisions of users'.

The use of the word 'material' means that the amount of the misstatement must be significant in relation to the size of the business. A misstatement of £1,000 in the financial statements of a small sole trader business could well be significant but, for a large limited company, will be less significant and unlikely to affect the decisions of users.

Examples of material misstatement and the economic consequences include:

- profit is overstated – may encourage investors to buy a stake of the business

- assets are overvalued – a lender may find that security for a loan is less than expected

- profit is understated – a lower amount of tax is paid to HM Revenue & Customs than should be paid

- sales turnover is overstated – more VAT is paid to HM Revenue & Customs than should be paid

APPLICATION OF ETHICAL PRINCIPLES WHEN PREPARING FINANCIAL STATEMENTS

When preparing financial statements, accounting staff must ensure that the statements are prepared accurately – without material misstatement – and in the public interest, without bias to any one user – for example, the owner(s). Behaving ethically is key to achieving this and consequently accounting staff should apply ethical principles when preparing financial statements.

The five fundamental ethical principles – as set out in AAT's Code of Professional Ethics – are:

- integrity – being straightforward and honest in all professional and business relationships

- objectivity – being aware of conflicts of interest and not allowing the influence of others to bias or override professional judgements

- professional competence and due care – maintaining professional knowledge and skill at the level required to ensure that an employer or client receives a competent service

- confidentiality – information should not be disclosed to third parties (unless permission has been given or there is a legal right or duty), and should be maintained securely at all times

- professional behaviour – ensuring that behaviour complies with relevant laws and regulations and avoids bringing the accountancy profession into disrepute

Examples of the application of ethical principles when preparing financial statements include:

- integrity – financial statements should not contain false or misleading figures or statements, or omit or obscure information so as to be misleading

- objectivity – the accountant is not influenced by the owner(s) who may want to manipulate the profit figure to suit their needs

- professional competence and due care – the accountant is up-to-date with current accounting standards and legal developments and carries out his/her work carefully, thoroughly and on a timely basis

- confidentiality – the profit and other information from the financial statements is not discussed with family and friends but only with the client and those work colleagues entitled to know

- professional behaviour – the accountant records all aspects of the preparation of financial statements in an honest and truthful way, in compliance with relevant laws and regulations

■ The primary users of financial statements include:
  - owner(s)/existing and potential investors
  - lenders
  - suppliers
  - employees
  - customers
  - government agencies
  - the public

■ The framework of accounting comprises:
  - accounting principles
  - accounting policies and characteristics
  - ethical principles

■ The accounting principles (or concepts) of business entity, materiality, going concern and accruals are fundamental to the relevance and reliability of financial records and statements.

■ The fundamental qualitative characteristics that make financial information useful are:
  - relevance
  - faithful representation

■ Supporting qualitative characteristics are:
  - comparability
  - verifiability
  - timeliness
  - understandability

■ Material misstatement is when information contained in the financial statements is untrue – whether accidentally or intentionally – and could influence the economic decisions of users.

■ The ethical principles to apply when preparing financial statements are:
  - integrity
  - objectivity
  - professional competence and due care
  - confidentiality
  - professional behaviour

Key Terms	**business entity principle**	financial statements record and report on the activities on one particular business
	materiality principle	items with a low value are not worthwhile recording in the accounts separately
	going concern principle	the presumption that the business to which the financial statements relate will continue to trade in the foreseeable future
	accruals principle	income and expenses are matched so that they relate to the same goods or services and the same accounting period
	relevance	fundamental qualitative accounting characteristic that requires financial information to be useful to users of financial statements
	faithful representation	fundamental qualitative accounting characteristic that requires financial information to correspond to the effect of transactions or events
	comparability	financial statements can be compared with those from previous years and with similar businesses
	verifiability	users of financial statements are assured that the information given is faithfully represented
	timeliness	users of financial statements receive information in time to enable decisions to be made
	understandability	financial information is presented clearly and concisely so that users can understand the information given

material misstatement	information contained in the financial statements is untrue – whether accidentally or intentionally
integrity	ethical principle of being straightforward and honest in all professional and business relationships
objectivity	ethical principle of being aware of conflicts of interest
professional competence and due care	ethical principle of maintaining professional knowledge and skill at the level required to provide a competent service to an employer or client
confidentiality	ethical principle that information should not be disclosed to third parties (unless permission is given or there is a legal duty), and should be maintained securely
professional behaviour	ethical principle of ensuring behaviour complies with relevant laws and regulations and does not bring the accountancy profession into disrepute

Activities

2.1   For the following three primary users of financial statements, identify how they might use the information contained in the statements:

User	Use of Information
Owner	
Lender	
Employee	

2.2   **(a)**   State the four important accounting principles (concepts).

   (b)   Explain how accounting principles help to make financial records and statements useful to users in the following contexts:

   –   internal control

   –   measuring business performance

   –   obtaining credit/financing

   –   statutory requirements

2.3   Write in the accounting principle (concept) which relates to each of the statements below.

Statement	Accounting Principle
Some items are of such low value that it is not worthwhile recording them separately.	
The financial statements record and report on the activities of one particular business.	
Income and expenses are matched so that they relate to the same goods or services and the same accounting period.	
The presumption is that the business to which the financial statements relate will continue to trade in the foreseeable future.	

2.4   **(a)**   State the two fundamental qualitative characteristics that make financial information useful.

1
2

(b)   Explain what is meant by each of the two fundamental qualitative characteristics.

2.5   There are four supporting qualitative characteristics that make financial information useful. From
       the following list, which are the **four** supporting characteristics?

(a) Verifiability	
(b) Materiality	
(c) Going concern	
(d) Timeliness	
(e) Understandability	
(f) Faithful representation	
(g) Comparability	
(h) Relevance	

2.6   **(a)**   Explain what is meant by 'material misstatement'.

       (b)   Give one example of the economic consequences to users of financial statements of the
                  following material misstatements:

Material misstatement	Economic consequence to users
Profit is overstated	
Assets are overvalued	
Sales turnover is overstated	

2.7 **(a)** State the five ethical principles to be followed when preparing financial statements.

(b) Identify the ethical principle involved in the following situations:

Situation	Relevant ethical principle
The owner of the business argues that expenses should be increased so as to show a lower profit figure.	
The financial statements show a misleading figure for depreciation so as to show a lower profit figure.	
The accounts trainee, who has only recently started in work, is given the financial statements to complete.	
Your friend, who works for the business whose financial statements you have just prepared, wants to know how much profit was made.	
The accountant preparing the financial statements works in an honest and truthful way.	

3 Preparing financial statements

this chapter covers...

In this chapter we look at the reasons for producing a trial balance and see how it is used in the preparation of financial statements (final accounts).

In previous studies you will have made extensive use of the extended trial balance format to show the statement of profit or loss and the statement of financial position.

The extended trial balance format gives an understanding of the principles of financial statements and it is often used by accountancy businesses as a first step towards preparing year end accounts for their clients. In this book we take the extended trial balance and develop it into the conventional format of financial statements as used by accountancy businesses.

We see the structure of the conventional format statement of profit or loss and statement of financial position and see the effect of the accounting equation on the financial statements.

At the end of the financial year, double-entry transfers are made so that items such as sales, purchases, expenses and closing inventory are closed off to the statement of profit or loss.

THE TRIAL BALANCE

The trial balance performs a check of the double-entry bookkeeping process. The reasons for producing a trial balance are:

- to check the accuracy of the double-entry
- to provide a starting point for the preparation of financial statements

You will remember from previous studies that, while the trial balance will reveal some errors in the double-entry, it will not reveal other errors. The following is a reminder of these errors.

errors not revealed by a trial balance

The following are the main errors that are not revealed by a trial balance:

- **error of principle**, where a transaction is entered in the wrong type of account
- **error of commission**, where a transaction is entered in the wrong account
- **error of original entry**, where the wrong amount is entered into both double-entry accounts
- **error of omission**, where a transaction is completely omitted from the double-entry accounts
- **reversal of entries**, where the debit and credit entries are made on the wrong side of both accounts

errors revealed by a trial balance

The trial balance will reveal errors in the double-entry such as:

- **one-sided entry**, where only one part of the two parts of a double-entry transaction has been recorded
- **entry duplicated on one side, nothing on the other**, where two debits or two credits have been recorded for a transaction
- **unequal entries**, where different amounts have been recorded for the debit and credit entries
- **account balance incorrectly transferred to the trial balance**, where the balance of an account is recorded incorrectly in the trial balance

limitations of a trial balance

Once errors have been corrected, the trial balance then provides the starting point for the preparation of year end financial statements. However, note the limitations of a trial balance:

- there may be errors in the double-entry bookkeeping that are not revealed by the trial balance

- amounts recorded in the trial balance do not distinguish between those that relate to the statement of profit or loss and those that relate to the statement of financial position

- the two-column trial balance does not give a profit figure – only when figures from the trial balance are used in the statement of profit or loss can profit be calculated

- closing inventory needs to be recognised in both the statement of profit or loss – as part of the calculation of cost of sales/cost of goods sold – and the statement of financial position as an adjustment to the trial balance

The bookkeeper's two-column trial balance is often developed into an extended trial balance. The extended trial balance gives an understanding of the principles of financial statements and is often used by accountancy businesses as a first step towards preparing year end accounts for their clients. The way in which accountants present financial statements is often described as being in the conventional format.

In the Case Study later in the chapter, we will use an extended trial balance to prepare year end financial statements, using the conventional format.

FINANCIAL STATEMENTS

Financial statements (final accounts) comprise:

- statement of profit or loss (sometimes referred to as an income statement)

- statement of financial position

Such financial statements can be produced more often than once a year in order to give information to the owner/owners on how the business is progressing. However, it is customary to produce annual accounts for the benefit of HM Revenue & Customs, lenders such as a bank, and other interested parties. In this way the statement of profit or loss covers an accounting period of a financial year (which can end at any date – it doesn't have to be the calendar year), and the statement of financial position shows the state of the business at the end of the accounting period.

STATEMENT OF PROFIT OR LOSS

income	minus	**expenses**	equals	**profit/loss**
revenue from sales		*costs of running the business*		*which adds/subtracts to/from capital/equity*

The statement of profit or loss shows the income a business has received over a given period for goods sold or services provided (together with any small amounts of other income, eg rent received). It also sets out the expenses incurred – the cost of the product, and the expenses (eg wages, administration expenses, rent, and so on). The difference between income and expenses is the profit for the year of the business. If expenses are greater than income, then a loss has been made. The profit (or loss) belongs to the owner/owners of the business. For a business that trades in goods, a figure for gross profit shows the profit made before expenses are deducted, and a profit for the year after expenses are deducted.

The format of a statement of profit or loss is as follows:

	Sales revenue
less	Cost of sales* (cost of purchases of goods, adjustment for change in inventories)
equals	**Gross profit**
less	Expenses (wages, administration expenses, rent, etc)
equals	**Profit for the year**

*often referred to as 'cost of goods sold'

Note that where an extended trial balance is being used, profit for the year can be checked against the figure shown in the ETB's statement of profit or loss columns.

Remember that, by transferring the balances of revenue and expense accounts to the statement of profit or loss, we are clearing those accounts ready for the start of the next financial year.

STATEMENT OF FINANCIAL POSITION

assets	minus	**liabilities**	equals	**capital/equity**
what a business owns		what a business owes		how the business has been financed

The statement of financial position uses the accounting equation to give a 'snapshot' of the business at a particular date – the end of the financial year. A typical business statement of financial position will show:

assets   What the business owns:

- non-current assets comprise the long-term items owned by a business:

  - intangible non-current assets which do not have material substance, eg goodwill (the amount paid for the reputation and connections of a business that has been bought – see page 121)

  - tangible non-current assets which have material substance, eg premises, vehicles, machinery, office equipment (shown at their carrying amount, ie cost price or revaluation less accumulated depreciation)

- current assets comprise short-term assets which change regularly, eg inventory held for resale, trade receivables, VAT repayable*, bank and cash balances (cash and cash equivalents)

liabilities   What the business owes:

- current liabilities, where payment is due within twelve months of the date of the statement of financial position, eg trade payables, bank overdraft, VAT payable*

- non-current liabilities, where payment is due in more than one year from the date of the statement of financial position, eg loans, mortgages, long-term bank loans

net assets   The total of non-current and current assets, less current and non-current liabilities. The net assets are financed by the owner/owners of the business, in the form of capital/equity. Net assets therefore equals the total of the 'financed by' section – the statement of financial position 'balances'.

capital/equity   Where the resources (eg money) to finance the business have come from – the investment of the owner/owners and business profits. The financial statements of limited companies use the term 'equity' in place of capital.

*Note that the balance of VAT control account can be either a current asset or a current liability in the statement of financial position:

– it is a current asset when a business is due a repayment of VAT from HM Revenue & Customs, eg where VAT paid on purchases and expenses exceeds VAT collected on sales, or where a business sells goods that are zero-rated for VAT (eg food, children's clothing) or exempt from VAT (eg postal services, loans of money)

– it is a current liability when a business owes the VAT it has collected on sales, less the VAT paid on purchases and expenses, to HM Revenue & Customs; this is the situation for most businesses

significance of the statement of financial position

The conventional format statement of financial position uses the accounting equation of assets minus liabilities equals capital/equity to show the assets used by the business and how they have been financed. The format is as follows:

	Non-current assets
plus	Net current assets (current assets – current liabilities)
minus	Non-current liabilities
equals	Net assets
equals	Capital/Equity

As financial transactions take place, they will change the statement of financial position and the equation – but the equation always balances.

For example, the purchase of a new machine on credit for use in the business has the following effect:

■ debit non-current assets (assets)

■ credit trade payables (liabilities)

When the machine is paid for from the bank the effect is:

■ debit trade payables (liabilities)

■ credit bank (asset, assuming that there is money in the bank)

If the business had a bank overdraft, the effect of paying for the machine would affect only the liabilities section of the statement of financial position:

■ debit trade payables (liabilities)

■ credit bank (liabilities)

In Activities and AAT Assessments you may well be asked to demonstrate your knowledge of the effect of business transactions on the accounting equation.

FROM ETB TO FINANCIAL STATEMENTS IN CONVENTIONAL FORMAT

situation

On the next page is the extended trial balance (ETB) of a business run by Tara Smith, who trades as 'The Fashion Shop'.

We will see how this ETB is used to prepare Tara Smith's financial statements, using the conventional format. We will prepare:

* the statement of profit or loss

* the statement of financial position

Note that the adjustments for closing inventory are already included in the ledger balance columns.

solution

The ETB does not present the financial statements in the conventional format, as used by accountants. While accountancy businesses often use the ETB as a first step, the figures have to be taken from the statement of profit or loss columns of the ETB and presented in vertical format – running down the page.

Tara Smith's statement of profit or loss is shown in conventional format on page 39. Study it carefully and see how the figures can be identified on the ETB on the next page. Note that the statement of profit or loss includes a figure for gross profit (because Tara's business trades in goods) which is the profit made before expenses are deducted, and a profit for the year after expenses are deducted.

Tara Smith's statement of financial position is shown in the conventional format on page 41. Study it carefully and see how the figures can be identified on the ETB shown on the next page.

EXTENDED TRIAL BALANCE TARA SMITH TRADING AS "THE FASHION SHOP" 31 DECEMBER 20-4

Account name	Ledger balances Dr £	Ledger balances Cr £	Adjustments Dr £	Adjustments Cr £	Statement of profit or loss Dr £	Statement of profit or loss Cr £	Statement of financial position Dr £	Statement of financial position Cr £
Opening inventory	12,500				12,500			
Purchases	105,000				105,000			
Sales revenue		155,000				155,000		
Administration expenses	6,200				6,200			
Wages	23,500				23,500			
Rent paid	750				750			
Telephone	500				500			
Interest paid	4,500				4,500			
Travel expenses	550				550			
Premises at cost	100,000						100,000	
Shop fittings at cost	20,000						20,000	
Sales ledger control	10,500						10,500	
Bank	5,450						5,450	
Cash	50						50	
Capital		75,000						75,000
Drawings	7,000						7,000	
Loan from bank		50,000						50,000
Purchases ledger control		14,500						14,500
Value Added Tax		2,000						2,000
Closing inventory – statement of profit or loss						10,500		
Closing inventory – statement of financial position	10,500						10,500	
Profit/loss for the year					12,000			12,000
	307,000	307,000			165,500	165,500	153,500	153,500

The **statement of profit or loss** includes a figure for gross profit because Tara Smith's business trades in goods. The statement of profit or loss finishes with profit for the year for the accounting period, ie profit after expenses.

The amounts for **sales revenue** and **purchases** include only items in which the business trades – eg a clothes shop buying clothes from the manufacturer and selling to the public. Note that any items bought for use in the business, such as a new till for the shop, are not included with purchases but are *capital expenditure* shown as assets on the statement of financial position.

Cost of sales, or cost of goods sold, represents the cost to the business of the goods which have been sold in this financial year. Cost of sales is:

	opening inventory	(inventory bought previously)
plus	purchases	(purchased during the year)
minus	closing inventory	(inventory left unsold at the end of the year)
equals	cost of sales	(cost of what has actually been sold)

Gross profit is calculated as:

sales revenue – cost of sales = gross profit

Expenses, or overheads, are the running costs of the business – known as *revenue expenditure.* The categories of expenses or overheads used vary according to the needs of each business.

Profit for the year is calculated as:

gross profit – expenses = profit for the year

If expenses are more than gross profit, the business has made a loss.

The profit for the year is the amount the business earned for the owner/owners, and is subject to taxation. The owner/owners can take some or all of the profit in the form of drawings. Part of the profit might well be left in the business in order to help build up the business for the future.

TARA SMITH, TRADING AS 'THE FASHION SHOP'

STATEMENT OF PROFIT OR LOSS
for the year ended 31 December 20-4

	£	£
Sales revenue		155,000
Opening inventory	12,500	
Purchases	105,000	
	117,500	
Less Closing inventory	10,500	
Cost of sales (Cost of goods sold)		107,000
Gross profit		48,000
Less expenses:		
Administration expenses	6,200	
Wages	23,500	
Rent paid	750	
Telephone	500	
Interest paid	4,500	
Travel expenses	550	
		36,000
Profit for the year		12,000

Non-current assets comprise the long-term items owned by a business:
- intangible non-current assets, which do not have material substance, eg goodwill (the amount paid for the reputation and connections of a business that has been bought)
- tangible non-current assets, which have material substance, eg premises, vehicles, machinery, office equipment (shown at their carrying amount)

Current assets comprise short-term assets which change regularly, eg inventory held for resale, trade receivables, bank balances and cash. These items will alter as the business trades, eg inventory will be sold, or more will be bought; trade receivables will make payment to the business, or sales on credit will be made; the cash and bank balances will alter with the flow of money in and out of the bank account.

Current liabilities are where payment is due within twelve months of the date of the statement of financial position, eg trade payables, and bank overdraft (which is usually repayable on demand, unlike a bank loan which is negotiated for a particular time period).

Net current assets is the excess of current assets over current liabilities, ie current assets – current liabilities = net current assets. Without adequate net current assets, a business will find it difficult to continue to operate. Net current assets is also often referred to as *working capital* .

Non-current liabilities are where payment is due in more than one year from the date of the statement of financial position; they are often described by terms such as loans, mortgages, long-term bank loans.

Net assets is the total of non-current and current assets, less current and non-current liabilities. The net assets are financed by the owner/owners of the business, in the form of capital or equity. Net assets therefore equals the total of the 'financed by' section – ie the statement of financial position 'balances'.

Capital is the investment of the owner/owners, and is a liability of a business, ie it is what the business owes the owner/owners. Opening capital + capital injection added during the year (if any) + profit for the year – drawings = closing capital (the investment of the owner/owners at the end of the year). For limited companies, equity is the term used in place of capital.

TARA SMITH, TRADING AS 'THE FASHION SHOP'

STATEMENT OF FINANCIAL POSITION

as at 31 December 20-4

	£	£	£
Non-current assets			
Premises			100,000
Shop fittings			20,000
			120,000
Current assets			
Inventory		10,500	
Trade receivables		10,500	
Bank		5,450	
Cash		50	
Total current assets		26,500	
Current liabilities			
Trade payables	14,500		
Value Added Tax	2,000		
Total current liabilities		16,500	
Net current assets			10,000
			130,000
Non-current liabilities			
Loan from bank			50,000
Net assets			80,000
Financed by:			
Capital			
Opening capital			75,000
Add Profit for the year			12,000
			87,000
Less Drawings			7,000
Closing capital			80,000

PREPARATION OF FINANCIAL STATEMENTS FROM A TRIAL BALANCE

The trial balance contains the basic figures necessary to prepare the year end financial statements. The information needed for the preparation of the financial statements is picked out from the trial balance in the following way:

- go through the trial balance and write against the items the financial statement in which each appears

- 'tick' each figure as it is used – each item from the trial balance appears in the financial statements once only

- here the closing inventory figure is listed in the trial balance, but may sometimes be shown as a note; you will remember that it appears twice in the financial statements – in the statement of profit or loss (as part of the calculation of cost of sales/cost of goods sold), and in the statement of financial position (as a current asset)

If this routine is followed with the trial balance of Tara Smith, it appears as follows:

Trial balance of Tara Smith as at 31 December 20-4				
	Dr £	Cr £		
Opening inventory	12,500		SPL (cost of sales)	✔
Purchases	105,000		SPL (cost of sales)	✔
Sales revenue		155,000	SPL (income)	✔
Administration expenses	6,200		SPL (expense)	✔
Wages	23,500		SPL (expense)	✔
Rent paid	750		SPL (expense)	✔
Telephone	500		SPL (expense)	✔
Interest paid	4,500		SPL (expense)	✔
Travel expenses	550		SPL (expense)	✔
Premises at cost	100,000		SFP (non-current asset)	✔
Shop fittings at cost	20,000		SFP (non-current asset)	✔
Sales ledger control	10,500		SFP (current asset)	✔
Bank	5,450		SFP (current asset)	✔
Cash	50		SFP (current asset)	✔
Capital		75,000	SFP (capital)	✔
Drawings	7,000		SFP (capital)	✔
Loan from bank		50,000	SFP (non-current liabs)	✔
Purchases ledger control		14,500	SFP (current liability)	✔
Value Added Tax		2,000	SFP (current liability)	✔
Closing inventory – statement of profit or loss		10,500	SPL (cost of sales)	✔
Closing inventory – statement of financial position	10,500		SFP (current asset)	✔
	307,000	307,000		

Note: SPL = statement of profit or loss; SFP - statement of financial position

In the trial balance illustrated here, items are grouped together – for example, all the statement of profit or loss expenses are listed together. This has been done to help you at these early stages in the preparation of conventional financial statements.

However, this grouping into categories will not always be the case. In particular, in Activities and Assessments, you will often find that the items listed in the trial balance appear in alphabetical order. This does have the effect of, for example, putting administration expenses (a statement of profit or loss expense) next to bank (which appears in the statement of financial position). It is time well spent to go through the trial balance carefully and to indicate where each item appears in the financial statements.

double-entry transfers for income and expenses

All of the items in the trial balance marked 'SPL' must be transferred to the statement of profit or loss by means of a double-entry transfer. Such items are for sales, purchases, expenses and closing inventory – the accounts are closed off at the end of the year by transfer to the statement of profit or loss. These accounts will then be ready to record business transactions in the next financial year.

Examples of double-entry transfers, using amounts from Tara Smith's trial balance are as follows:

income account

Dr			Sales revenue account		Cr
20-4		£	20-4		£
31 Dec	*Statement of profit or loss	155,000	31 Dec	Balance b/d	155,000
	amount transferred to statement of profit or loss			amount shown in the trial balance	

cost of sales and expenses accounts

Dr			Purchases account		Cr
20-4		£	20-4		£
31 Dec	Balance b/d	105,000	31 Dec	*Statement of profit or loss	105,000
	amount shown in the trial balance			amount transferred to statement of profit or loss	

*Note that, alternatively, the cross-reference may be written as 'Profit or loss account'.

Dr		Administration expenses account		Cr
20-4		£	20-4	£
31 Dec	Balance b/d	6,200	31 Dec Statement of profit or loss	6,200
	amount shown in the trial balance		amount transferred to statement of profit or loss	

All other expenses accounts – in Tara Smith's trial balance for wages, rent paid, telephone, interest paid and travel expenses – are closed off by transfer to the statement of profit or loss in the same way.

inventory account

Dr		Inventory account		Cr
20-4		£	20-4	£
31 Dec	Balance b/d	12,500	31 Dec Statement of profit or loss	12,500
31 Dec	Statement of profit or loss	10,500		
	the closing inventory of £10,500 is debited here and recorded on the statement of profit or loss; the amount of inventory is an asset which is shown on the statement of financial position		the opening inventory of £12,500 is transferred to the statement of profit or loss	

Note that there are other ways of accounting for closing inventory: a cost of sales account can be used (see page 90), or separate accounts can be used for opening and closing inventory.

profit and drawings

Profit for the year and the amount of drawings relate to the owner/owners of the business. The amounts are transferred to capital account as follows:

Dr		Capital account		Cr
20-4		£	20-4	£
31 Dec	Drawings	7,000	31 Dec Balance b/d	75,000
31 Dec	Balance c/d	80,000	31 Dec Profit for the year	12,000
		87,000		87,000
20-5			20-5	
			1 Jan Balance b/d	80,000
			£80,000 is the amount of closing capital on the statement of financial position (see page 41)	

assets and liabilities

All of the remaining items from the trial balance form the assets and liabilities of the statement of financial position. The account balances are carried forward into next year's financial statements.

The balance of capital account is shown in the 'financed by' section where it is usual to show the following:

	Opening capital
add	Profit for the year
less	Drawings
equals	Closing capital

FINANCIAL STATEMENTS: POINTS TO NOTE

assets and the order of liquidity

In the statement of financial position it is customary to list the assets – non-current assets and current assets – in an 'increasing order of liquidity'. In accounting, liquidity means nearness to cash, so the most permanent assets – ie those that are furthest away from cash – are listed first. Thus premises, which would take time to turn into cash, heads the list, with other non-current assets – such as shop fittings, machinery and vehicles – following. For current assets, the usual order is to start with inventory, then trade receivables, bank (if not overdrawn), and cash. In this way, the assets are listed from the most permanent (usually premises) to the most liquid (cash itself).

The reason for this order is historical – nineteenth-century business owners wanted to impress upon readers of their financial statements the solid assets that they owned. The top line of the balance sheet (as the statement of financial position was known then) was the first to be read and that showed the value of their premises. The following lines listed their other assets. This traditional approach lives on into twenty-first century financial statements.

adjustments to financial statements

Whilst the starting point for the preparation of financial statements is the bookkeeper's two-column trial balance, if we used only the trial balance figures (which record the financial transactions that have taken place) the resultant financial statements would show an inaccurate picture of the state of the business. Adjustments are made with the aim of improving the accuracy of the financial statements in showing the profit, and the assets and liabilities of the business.

The main adjustments to financial statements are for:

■ closing inventory

■ accruals and prepayments of expenses and income

■ depreciation of non-current assets

■ irrecoverable debts written off

■ allowance for doubtful debts

In Chapter 5 we see how these adjustments affect the conventional format financial statements.

FINANCIAL STATEMENTS: LAYOUT

A layout or pro-forma for financial statements is included in the Appendix. This may be photocopied (it is advisable to enlarge it up to A4 size); alternatively, the layout can be downloaded from the website www.osbornebooks.co.uk. It shows:

– a statement of profit or loss

– a statement of financial position

Note that when used for partnership financial statements (see Chapter 6), the layout will need to be adjusted to take note of the appropriation of profits and of the partners' capital and current accounts.

FURTHER ITEMS IN FINANCIAL STATEMENTS

There are a number of further double-entry items that may have to be incorporated into the statement of profit or loss. These items include:

■ carriage in

■ carriage out

■ sales returns

■ purchases returns

■ discounts received

■ discounts allowed

carriage in

This is the expense to a buyer of the carriage (transport) costs. For example, if an item is purchased on the internet, the buyer may have to pay the additional cost of delivery.

In a statement of profit or loss, the cost of carriage in is added to the cost of purchases. The reason for doing this is so that all purchases are at a 'delivered to the door' price.

carriage out

This is where the seller pays the expense of the carriage charge. For example, an item is sold to the customer and described as 'post free' or 'carriage free'.

In the statement of profit or loss, the cost of carriage out on sales is shown as an expense of the business.

sales returns

Sales returns (or *returns in*) is where a credit customer returns goods to the business.

In conventional format financial statements, the amount of sales returns is deducted from the figure for sales revenue in the statement of profit or loss.

purchases returns

Purchases returns (or *returns out*) is where a business returns goods to a supplier.

In conventional format financial statements, the amount of purchases returns is deducted from the figure for purchases in the statement of profit or loss.

discounts received

Discounts received is an allowance offered by suppliers on purchases invoice amounts for prompt payment, eg 2% discount for prompt payment within seven days.

In financial statements, the amount of discounts received is shown in the statement of profit or loss as income received.

discounts allowed

Discounts allowed is an allowance offered to customers on sales invoice amounts for prompt payment.

In financial statements, the amount of discounts allowed is shown in the statement of profit or loss as an expense.

Case Study

STATEMENT OF PROFIT OR LOSS – FURTHER ITEMS

situation

An extract from the trial balance of Natasha Morgan is as follows:

Trial balance (extract) as at 30 June 20-8

	Dr £	Cr £
Opening inventory	12,350	
Sales revenue		250,000
Purchases	156,000	
Sales returns	5,400	
Purchases returns		7,200
Carriage in	1,450	
Carriage out	3,250	
Discounts received		2,500
Discounts allowed	3,700	
Other expenses	78,550	
Closing inventory – statement of profit or loss		16,300

Natasha asks for your help in the preparation of her statement of profit or loss, using the conventional format.

solution

There are a number of further items to be incorporated into the layout of the statement of profit or loss. In particular, the calculation of cost of sales/cost of goods sold is made in the following way:

opening inventory
+ purchases
+ carriage in
– purchases returns
– closing inventory
= cost of sales

The statement of profit or loss for Natasha Morgan's business is shown on the next page. Note the use of three money columns.

NATASHA MORGAN
STATEMENT OF PROFIT OR LOSS
for the year ended 30 June 20-8

	£	£	£
Sales revenue			250,000
Less Sales returns			5,400
Net sales revenue			244,600
Opening inventory		12,350	
Purchases	156,000		
Add Carriage in	1,450		
	157,450		
Less Purchases returns	7,200		
Net purchases		150,250	
		162,600	
Less Closing inventory		16,300	
Cost of sales			146,300
Gross profit			98,300
Add income: Discounts received			2,500
			100,800
Less expenses:			
Discounts allowed		3,700	
Carriage out		3,250	
Other expenses		78,550	
			85,500
Profit for the year			15,300

SERVICE SECTOR BUSINESSES

The financial statements of a service sector business – such as a secretarial agency, solicitor, estate agent, doctor – do not normally include a calculation of gross profit. This is because the business, instead of trading in goods, supplies services.

The statement of profit or loss commences with the income from the business activity – such as 'fees', 'income from clients', 'charges', 'work done'. Other items of income – such as discount received – are added, and the expenses are then listed and deducted to give the profit or (loss) for the year. An example of a service sector statement of profit or loss is shown below:

JEMMA SMITH, TRADING AS 'WYVERN SECRETARIAL AGENCY'
STATEMENT OF PROFIT OR LOSS
for the year ended 31 December 20-8

	£	£
Income from clients		110,000
Less expenses:		
Salaries	64,000	
Heating and lighting	2,000	
Telephone	2,000	
Rent and rates	6,000	
Sundry expenses	3,000	
		77,000
Profit for the year		33,000

The layout of the statement of financial position for a service sector business is identical to that seen earlier; the only difference is that there is unlikely to be much, if any, inventory in the current assets section.

Chapter Summary	■	The trial balance provides:

■ The trial balance provides:

– an initial check of the accuracy of the double-entry bookkeeping

– the starting point for the preparation of year end financial statements

■ The extended trial balance (ETB) format is a first step towards preparing year end financial statements. From the ETB can be developed financial statements in the conventional format used by accountants.

■ In the conventional format, the financial statements of a sole trader comprise:

– statement of profit or loss (which may include a figure for gross profit)

– statement of financial position

■ Further bookkeeping items incorporated into financial statements include:

– carriage in

– carriage out

– sales returns

– purchases returns

– discounts received

– discounts allowed

Key Terms

conventional format	the form of financial statements used by accountants
gross profit	sales revenue minus cost of sales, ie the profit made before expenses are deducted
profit for the year	gross profit minus expenses, ie the profit which belongs to the owner/owners of the business
assets	items owned by the business, split between non-current assets and current assets
liabilities	items owed by the business, split between current liabilities and non-current liabilities
capital/equity	the investment of the owner/owners in the business
service sector business	a business which supplies services, eg secretarial agency, solicitor, estate agent

Activities

Blank photocopiable layouts of the statement of profit or loss and the statement of financial position are included in the Appendix – it is advisable to enlarge them up to A4 size.

3.1 This Activity is about calculating missing balances and the accounting equation.

You are given the following information about a business as at 1 April 20-6:

The value of assets and liabilities was:

- Non-current assets at carrying amount   £21,500
- Trade receivables   £8,750
- Bank (overdrawn)   £1,290
- Trade payables   £5,480

There were no other assets or liabilities.

(a) Calculate the capital account balance as at 1 April 20-6.

£ [   ]

(b) On 30 April 20-6, a new vehicle is purchased on credit for use in the business. Tick the boxes to show what effect this transaction will have on the balances. You must choose **one** answer for **each** line.

	Debit	**Credit**	**No change**
Non-current assets			
Trade receivables			
Trade payables			
Bank			
Capital			

(c) Which of the following is best described as a current liability? Tick **one** answer.

(a) A bank loan repayable in two years' time	
(b) A bank overdraft	
(c) Drawings by the owner of the business	
(d) Inventory sold and awaiting collection by the customer	

3.2 The following trial balance has been extracted by Nick Johnson on 31 December 20-3:

	Dr £	Cr £
Opening inventory	25,000	
Purchases	210,000	
Sales revenue		310,000
Administration expenses	12,400	
Wages	41,000	
Rent paid	7,500	
Telephone	1,000	
Interest paid	9,000	
Travel expenses	1,100	
Premises at cost	200,000	
Machinery at cost	40,000	
Sales ledger control	31,000	
Bank	900	
Cash	100	
Capital		150,000
Drawings	14,000	
Loan from bank		100,000
Purchases ledger control		29,000
Value Added Tax		4,000
Closing inventory – statement of profit or loss		21,000
Closing inventory – statement of financial position	21,000	
	614,000	614,000

You are to prepare the financial statements of Nick Johnson for the year ended 31 December 20-3, using the conventional format.

3.3 The following trial balance has been extracted by the bookkeeper of Alan Harris at 30 June 20-4:

	Dr	Cr
	£	£
Opening inventory	13,250	
Capital		70,000
Premises at cost	65,000	
Vehicle at cost	5,250	
Purchases	55,000	
Sales revenue		85,500
Administration expenses	850	
Wages	9,220	
Rent paid	1,200	
Telephone	680	
Interest paid	120	
Travel expenses	330	
Sales ledger control	1,350	
Purchases ledger control		6,400
Value Added Tax		1,150
Bank	2,100	
Cash	600	
Drawings	8,100	
Closing inventory – statement of profit or loss		18,100
Closing inventory – statement of financial position	18,100	
	181,150	181,150

You are to prepare the financial statements of Alan Harris for the year ended 30 June 20-4, using the conventional format.

3.4 An extract from the trial balance of Christine Lorraine is as follows:

Trial balance (extract) as at 30 June 20-1

	Dr	Cr
	£	£
Opening inventory	15,140	
Sales revenue		175,000
Purchases	102,000	
Sales returns	4,100	
Purchases returns		8,300
Carriage in	1,210	
Carriage out	5,680	
Discounts received		790
Discounts allowed	1,460	
Other expenses	58,230	
Closing inventory – statement of profit or loss		18,350

You are to prepare the statement of profit or loss of Christine Lorraine for the year ended 30 June 20-1, using the conventional format.

4 Incomplete records accounting

this chapter covers...

In the last chapter we saw how financial statements are prepared from double-entry accounts, together with the production of a trial balance. However, there are a number of circumstances when full double-entry accounts are not available – the business may not keep adequate records, or information may have been lost as a result of a disaster such as a fire or a flood, or there may be differences between the accounts. Whatever the circumstances, some financial information – incomplete records – will be available and, at the end of the year, it is the task of the accountant to construct the financial statements from these.

This chapter looks at

■ *the information available when constructing financial statements from incomplete records*

■ *how information that is required can be calculated*

■ *preparing year end financial statements from incomplete records*

■ *the use of gross profit mark-up and margin in incomplete records accounting*

WHAT ARE INCOMPLETE RECORDS?

Incomplete records is the term used where some aspect of the accounting system is missing.

Incomplete records occurs when:

- information has been lost as a result of a disaster – such as a fire, a flood – or the theft or loss of books or ledgers, including records held on computer
- there are inadequate or missing accounting records, for example concerning purchases, sales, trade payables, and trade receivables
- there are differences between
  - the ledger accounts, non-current asset register and the physical non-current assets held by the business
  - the business' inventory records, inventory total and the physical inventory count held by the business
  - the business cash book and the bank statement received from the bank
  - the purchases ledger accounts and statements received from suppliers
- timing differences, for examples where goods have been ordered but not yet received, or where payments made for purchases have been sent but are not yet recorded on the bank account

The task of the accountant faced with incomplete records is to construct the financial statements by:

- using the information that is available
- seeing what information is not available, and how 'missing' figures can be calculated

information available to the accountant

The basic financial record kept by most businesses is a cash book which records the business cash and bank transactions. Often the cash book is operated on the **single-entry** system, ie there is no double-entry. In practice, even if a cash book has not been kept, it is usually possible to reconstruct it from banking records, although this task can prove to be time-consuming. Other financial information will be available so that, in all, the accountant has the following to work from:

- cash book – the basic record for any single entry system
- banking details – statements, paying-in books, cheque stubs and other bank transfers
- invoices – both invoices received (for purchases) and copies of invoices sent (for sales) during the year
- expenses – during the year
- lists of amounts owing to suppliers (trade payables), and due from customers (trade receivables), at the beginning and end of the year
- assets and liabilities – non-current and current assets, long-term and current liabilities, at the beginning and end of the year
- non-current assets – bought or sold during the year

Information which may not be available, and will need to be calculated includes:

- capital at the beginning of the year
- purchases and sales for the year
- cash book summary for the year
- profit or loss for the year
- drawings for the year

acting with integrity

It is important that accounting staff preparing financial statements must always act with integrity. This means that they must be straightforward and honest in all professional and business relationships.

the tools of accounting

From the two Case Studies which follow (on pages 59 and 66) we will see how to take the financial information that is available and, using the tools of accounting, to construct the accounts that are required. The tools of accounting that may be needed are:

- the use of an opening trial balance, or statement of assets and liabilities
- the construction of a cash account and/or bank account
- the use of control accounts – sales ledger control account, purchases ledger control account and VAT control account (or sales tax control account)
- the preparation of financial statements – statement of profit or loss and statement of financial position

In addition, the following may be of use:

- the accounting equation (assets − liabilities = capital/equity)
- gross profit mark-up and margin (see page 72)

The two Case Studies make use of these tools of accounting, although it should be emphasised that no two incomplete records situations are the same; however practice will help to develop your skills in this aspect of accounts preparation.

Case Study

JAYNE PERRY – STATIONERY SUPPLIES

The following information has been taken from the incomplete records of Jayne Perry, who runs a small stationery supplies business.

LIST OF ASSETS AND LIABILITIES		
	1 Jan 20-4	**31 Dec 20-4**
	£	£
Shop fittings	8,000	8,000
Inventory	25,600	29,800
Trade receivables	29,200	20,400
Bank (money at the bank)	5,000	not known
Trade payables	20,800	16,000
Administration expenses owing	200	300

BANK SUMMARY FOR 20-4	
	£
Receipts from trade receivables	127,800
Payments to trade payables	82,600
Drawings	12,500
Administration expenses	30,600

In the text which follows we shall see how Jayne Perry's accountant will construct the financial statements for 20-4 from incomplete records. The information to be calculated is:

- opening capital, at the beginning of the financial year
- cash book summary for the year
- purchases and sales for the year
- profit or loss for the year, and a year end statement of financial position

Note: for the sake of simplicity we will ignore VAT on all transactions in this Case Study.

OPENING CAPITAL

Opening capital is needed because a year end statement of financial position is to be prepared. In other situations with incomplete records, opening capital may be known, being the difference between assets and liabilities. To calculate the capital at the beginning of the financial year, we use the accounting equation: *assets – liabilities = capital*.

This is presented as a **statement of assets and liabilities** as follows:

	£	£
JAYNE PERRY		
STATEMENT OF ASSETS AND LIABILITIES		
as at 1 January 20-4		
Assets		
Shop fittings		8,000
Inventory		25,600
Trade receivables		29,200
Bank		5,000
		67,800
Less Liabilities		
Trade payables	20,800	
Administration expenses owing	200	
		21,000
Capital at 1 January 20-4		46,800

Notes:

▪ here, the bank balance is an asset, ie money in the bank; if it was marked as an overdraft, it would be included amongst the liabilities

▪ look out for the opening bank balance or overdraft being stated elsewhere in the information; for example, a bank summary may be given which starts with the bank figure at the beginning of the year – this figure must be included in the statement of assets and liabilities, which is used to calculate opening capital

CASH BOOK SUMMARY

A cash book/bank summary enables us to find out the cash and bank balances at the year end. (Sometimes this is not necessary, as a cash book may have been prepared already by the owner of the business.) In practice, the entries on the bank statement can be used to produce a summary of bank receipts and payments for the year. In the case of Jayne Perry's business, the cash book (bank columns) are:

Dr			**Cash book (bank columns)**		Cr
20-4		£	20-4		£
1 Jan	Balance b/d	5,000		Payments to trade	
	Receipts from trade			payables	82,600
	receivables	127,800		Drawings	12,500
				Administration expenses	30,600
			31 Dec	Balance c/d	7,100
		132,800			132,800
20-5			20-5	**missing figure**	
1 Jan	Balance b/d	7,100			

The bank balance of £7,100 on 31 December 20-4 is calculated by filling in the missing figure.

Notes:

- when preparing a cash book summary, look out for an opening bank balance that is **overdrawn**; this is entered on the credit side
- at the end of the cash book summary, a credit balance brought down is an overdraft
- if working from a bank statement, take care with the balances. Remember that a credit balance at the bank (money in the bank) is a debit balance in the business accounts, which represents an asset of the business. By contrast a debit balance at the bank (an overdraft) is a credit balance in the business accounts, which represents a liability of the business

PURCHASES AND SALES

In calculating purchases and sales, we need to take note of the trade payables and trade receivables at both the beginning and the end of the year. The important point to note is that payments are **not** the same as purchases for the year (because of the change in the level of trade payables). Likewise, receipts are not the same as sales (because of the change in trade receivables). Only in a business which trades solely on cash terms and has no trade receivables and trade payables would the receipts and payments be the figures for sales and purchases.

calculating purchases and sales

The method of calculating the purchases and sales figures is:

- **purchases for year** = payments in year, *less* trade payables at the beginning of the year, *plus* trade payables at the end of the year
- **sales for year** = receipts in year, *less* trade receivables at the beginning of the year, *plus* trade receivables at the end of the year

When calculating purchases and sales, also take note of any purchases returns and sales returns, any cash (settlement) discounts received and discounts allowed, and – for sales – irrecoverable debts (but ignore an allowance for doubtful debts), contra transactions (eg set offs between sales ledger and purchases ledger) and goods taken for own use by the owner of the business.

The figures from Jayne Perry's business are:

purchases	= £82,600 – £20,800 + £16,000	= £77,800
sales	= £127,800 – £29,200 + £20,400	= £119,000

use of control accounts

The use of control accounts is recommended for calculating purchases and sales in incomplete records. We can use the information for purchases given in the Case Study as follows:

Dr			**Purchases ledger control account**		Cr
20-4		£	20-4		£
	Payments to trade		1 Jan	Balance b/d	20,800
	payables	82,600		Purchases *(missing figure)*	?
31 Dec	Balance c/d	16,000			
		98,600			98,600
20-5			20-5		
			1 Jan	Balance b/d	16,000

The missing figure of purchases for the year is calculated as:

£98,600 – £20,800 = £77,800

In a similar way, the sales figure can be calculated:

Dr	Sales ledger control account			Cr
20-4	£	20-4		£
1 Jan Balance b/d	29,200	Receipts from trade		
Sales *(missing figure)*	?	receivables	127,800	
		31 Dec Balance c/d	20,400	
	148,200		148,200	
20-5		20-5		
1 Jan Balance b/d	20,400			

The missing figure of sales for the year is £148,200 – £29,200 = £119,000

Note that, where the owner of the business has taken goods for own use, the figures for sales and drawings will need to be increased (credit sales account; debit drawings account).

The control account method, although its use is not essential in incomplete records accounting, does bring a discipline to calculating the two important figures of purchases and sales. Do not forget that the control accounts give the figures for **credit** purchases and sales: cash purchases and sales need to be added, where applicable, to obtain total purchases and sales for the year.

purchases and sales – summary

Whichever method of calculating purchases or sales is used – calculation, or a control account – four pieces of information are usually required:

- opening balance
- closing balance
- bank and cash payments or receipts for the year
- purchases or sales for the year

Provided that any three are known, the fourth can be calculated – the figure for purchases and sales was missing from the examples above. However if, for example, we know the opening and closing trade receivables totals, together with sales for the year, then it is a simple matter to calculate the missing figure for receipts from trade receivables.

Remember that, if they are applicable, purchases returns and sales returns, cash (settlement) discounts received and discounts allowed, and – for sales – irrecoverable debts (credit sales ledger control), should also be incorporated into the control accounts.

When calculating purchases and sales be aware that irrelevant data might be given in Activities and AAT Assessments – eg for sales, reference to an allowance for doubtful debts.

VAT control account

Note that a VAT control account (or sales tax control account) may be needed for VAT-registered businesses – see page 69 of the next Case Study. Also, with incomplete records, be ready to make VAT calculations to extract net or VAT from a gross figure which includes VAT.

PREPARATION OF THE FINANCIAL STATEMENTS

statement of profit or loss

Having calculated the figures for purchases and sales, we can now prepare the statement of profit or loss. The section as far as gross profit is:

JAYNE PERRY		
STATEMENT OF PROFIT OR LOSS		
for the year ended 31 December 20-4		
	£	£
Sales revenue		119,000
Opening inventory	25,600	
Purchases	77,800	
	103,400	
Less Closing inventory	29,800	
Cost of sales		73,600
Gross profit		45,400

The expenses section of the statement of profit or loss follows but, before we are able to complete this, we need to know the figure for administration expenses for the year. The relevant information from the Case Study is:

- bank payments for administration expenses during year, £30,600

- administration expenses owing at 1 January 20-4, £200

- administration expenses owing at 31 December 20-4, £300

Like the calculation of purchases and sales, we cannot simply use the bank payments figure for expenses; we must take note of cash payments, together with accruals (and prepayments). The calculation is:

expenses for year = bank and cash payments, *less* accruals at the beginning of the year (or *plus* prepayments), *plus* accruals at the end of the year (or *less* prepayments)

Thus the figure for Jayne Perry's administration expenses is:

£30,600 – £200 + £300 = £30,700.

Alternatively, the figure can be calculated by means of a control account:

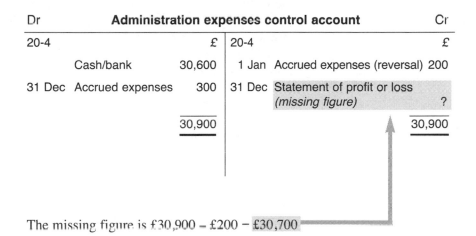

Dr		**Administration expenses control account**		Cr
20-4		£	20-4	£
	Cash/bank	30,600	1 Jan Accrued expenses (reversal)	200
31 Dec	Accrued expenses	300	31 Dec Statement of profit or loss (missing figure)	?
		30,900		30,900

The missing figure is £30,900 – £200 – £30,700

Jayne Perry's statement of profit or loss concludes as follows:

	£
Gross profit	45,400
Less expenses:	
Administration expenses	30,700
Profit for the year	14,700

statement of financial position

The statement of financial position can now be prepared using the assets and liabilities from the Case Study.

JAYNE PERRY
STATEMENT OF FINANCIAL POSITION
as at 31 December 20-4

	£	£	£
Non-current assets			
Shop fittings			8,000
Current assets			
Inventory		29,800	
Trade receivables		20,400	
Bank		7,100	
Total current assets		57,300	
Current liabilities			
Trade payables	16,000		
Accrual of administration expenses	300		
Total current liabilities		16,300	
Net current assets			41,000
Net assets			49,000
Financed by:			
Capital			£
Opening capital			46,800
Add Profit for the year			14,700
			61,500
Less Drawings			12,500
Closing capital			49,000

ELECTROPARTS

We will now look at a more comprehensive example of incomplete records accounting. This incorporates sales returns, VAT (including the use of VAT control account), depreciation and the sale of a non-current asset, and concludes with the preparation of financial statements. You may like to work through the Case Study before comparing your solution with the one shown.

situation

John Anstey owns a small business, Electroparts, which supplies spare parts for a wide range of electrical goods – cookers, fridges, freezers, kettles, dishwashers, etc.

His customers are self-employed repairers who buy parts for specific jobs from his trade counter – John allows them credit terms. There are no cash sales. All purchases made by John from suppliers are on credit terms.

All sales, disposals of assets and purchases are standard-rated for VAT at 20%.

John does not keep a full set of accounting records; however, the following information has been produced for the year ended 31 March 20-8:

Assets and Liabilities of Electroparts at 1 April 20-7

		£	£
ASSETS	Fixtures and fittings at cost		15,000
	Less accumulated depreciation		7,500
			7,500
	Inventory	24,400	
	Trade receivables	21,650	
	Prepayment of administration expenses	140	
			46,190
	TOTAL ASSETS		53,690
LIABILITIES	Trade payables	15,950	
	Value Added Tax	2,310	
	Bank	12,850	
	TOTAL LIABILITIES		31,110
CAPITAL			22,580

Bank account summary for the year ended 31 March 20-8

	£		£
Trade receivables	207,410	Balance b/d	12,850
Disposal of fixtures		Trade payables	139,620
and fittings (inc VAT)	1,950	Administration expenses	17,760
		Wages	18,280
		HMRC for VAT	4,360
		Drawings	15,390
		Balance c/d	1,100
	209,360		209,360

Day book summaries for the year	Net £	VAT £	Total £
Sales	196,400	39,280	235,680
Sales returns	1,560	312	1,872
Purchases	135,600	27,120	162,720
Administration expenses	14,800	2,960	17,760
Note: there were no purchases returns during the year			

Further information:

– On 31 March 20-8, inventory was valued at £28,400

– Cash (settlement) discounts received during the year totalled £760; there was no cash discount allowed during the year

– Depreciation is charged at the rate of 10% on the cost of fixtures and fittings held at the end of the financial year. No depreciation is charged in the year of disposal

– Fixtures and fittings purchased on 1 April 20-5 for £2,500 (net of VAT) were sold on 30 September 20-7 for £1,950 (including VAT)

– On 31 March 20-8, £210 was owing for administration expenses

John Anstey asks you to:

1 Calculate the amount of trade receivables at 31 March 20-8

2 Calculate the amount of trade payables at 31 March 20-8

3 Calculate the gain or loss on the disposal of fixtures and fittings

4 Calculate the amount of VAT due to HM Revenue & Customs at 31 March 20-8

5 Calculate the amount of administration expenses to be shown in the statement of profit or loss for the year ended 31 March 20-8

6 Prepare the statement of profit or loss for the year ended 31 March 20-8

7 Prepare the statement of financial position at 31 March 20-8

solution

1

Dr		Sales ledger control account			Cr
20-7/-8		£	20-7/-8		£
1 Apr	Balance b/d	21,650		Sales returns day book	1,872
	Sales day book	235,680		Bank	207,410
			31 Mar	Balance c/d *(missing figure)*	48,048
		257,330			257,330

2

Dr		Purchases ledger control account			Cr
20-7/-8		£	20-7/-8		£
	Bank	139,620	1 Apr	Balance b/d	15,950
	Discounts received	760		Purchases day book	162,720
31 Mar	Balance c/d *(missing figure)*	38,290			
		178,670			178,670

3

Gain or loss on disposal of fixtures and fittings

Depreciation charge per year	£250
Number of years' depreciation	2 (20-5/-6,20-6/-7; no depreciation in year of sale)
Accumulated depreciation	£500
Disposals	£1,625 + £325 VAT = £1,950

Dr			**Disposals account**		Cr
20-7/-8		£	20-7/-8		£
30 Sep	Fixtures and fittings	2,500	30 Sep	Accumulated depreciation	500
30 Sep	VAT on disposals	325	30 Sep	Bank (disposal proceeds)	1,950
			31 Mar	Statement of profit or loss (loss on disposal)	375
		2,825			2,825

4

Dr		**VAT control account**			Cr
20 7/ 8		£	20 7/ 8		£
	Sales returns day book	312	1 Apr	Balance b/d	2,310
	Purchases day book	27,120		Sales day book	39,280
	Administration expenses day book	2,980		Disposals	325
	Bank	4,360			
31 Mar	Balance c/d (missing figure)	7,163			
		41,915			41,915

5

Dr		**Administration expenses control account**			Cr
20-7/-8		£	20-7/-8		£
1 Apr	Prepaid expenses (reversal)	140	31 Mar	Statement of profit or loss (missing figure)	15,150
	Administration expenses day book	*14,800			
31 Mar	Accrued expenses	210			
		15,150			15,150
	* net of VAT				

6

JOHN ANSTEY, TRADING AS 'ELECTROPARTS'
STATEMENT OF PROFIT OR LOSS
for the year ended 31 March 20-8

	£	£
Sales revenue		196,400
Less Sales returns		1,560
Net sales		194,840
Opening inventory	24,400	
Purchases	135,600	
	160,000	
Less Closing inventory	28,400	
Cost of sales		131,600
Gross profit		63,240
Add income: Discounts received		760
		64,000
Less expenses:		
Administration expenses	15,150	
Loss on disposal of fixtures and fittings	375	
Depreciation charge: fixtures and fittings	*1,250	
Wages	18,280	
		35,055
Profit for the year		28,945

*Note	
Fixtures and fittings at cost on 1 April 20-7	£15,000
Less cost price of fixtures and fittings sold 30 September 20-7	£2,500
Fixtures and fittings at cost on 31 March 20-8	£12,500
Depreciation charge at 10%	£1,250

7

JOHN ANSTEY, TRADING AS 'ELECTROPARTS'
STATEMENT OF FINANCIAL POSITION
as at 31 March 20-8

Non-current assets	Cost	Accumulated depreciation	Carrying amount
	£	£	£
Fixtures and fittings	12,500	*8,250	4,250

Current assets		
Inventory		28,400
Trade receivables		48,048
Bank		1,100
Total current assets		77,548

Current liabilities		
Trade payables	38,290	
Value Added Tax	7,163	
Accrual of administration expenses	210	
Total current liabilities		45,663
Net current assets		31,885
Net assets		36,135

Financed by:	
Capital	£
Opening capital (from assets and liabilities at 1 April 20-7)	22,580
Add Profit for the year	28,945
	51,525
Less Drawings	15,390
Closing capital	36,135

***Note**	
Accumulated depreciation of fixtures and fittings at 1 April 20-7	7,500
Less accumulated depreciation on asset sold	500
	7,000
Depreciation charge for year (see statement of profit or loss)	1,250
Accumulated depreciation of fixtures and fittings at 31 March 20-8	8,250

THE USE OF GROSS PROFIT MARK-UP AND MARGIN

It is often necessary to use accounting ratios and percentages/fractions in the preparation of financial statements from incomplete records.

The two main percentages/fractions used for incomplete records accounting are:

■ gross profit mark-up

■ gross profit margin (or gross sales margin)

It is quite common for a business to establish its selling price by reference to either a mark-up or a margin. The difference between the two is that:

■ mark-up is a profit percentage or fraction added to **buying** or **cost** price

■ margin is a profit percentage or fraction based on the **selling** price

For example, a product is bought by a retailer at a cost of £100; the retailer sells it for £125, ie

cost price + gross profit = selling price

£100 + £25 = £125

The *mark-up* is:

$$\frac{\text{gross profit}}{\text{cost price}} \times \frac{100}{1} = \frac{£25}{£100} \times \frac{100}{1} = \textbf{25\%/one-quarter}$$

The *margin* (or *gross sales margin*) is:

$$\frac{\text{gross profit}}{\text{selling price}} \times \frac{100}{1} = \frac{£25}{£125} \times \frac{100}{1} = \textbf{20\%/one-fifth}$$

Note that, where a business is registered for VAT, mark-up and margin are calculated on cost and selling prices that are net of VAT. With VAT at 20%, multiply by five-sixths for the net of VAT amount: eg sales of £120 including VAT, multiplied by five-sixths, is £100 net of VAT.

In incomplete records accounting, mark-up or the margin percentages can be used in a range of circumstances, as shown by the examples which follow.

Worked examples

example 1 – calculation of sales

- Cost of sales is £150,000
- Mark-up is 40%

What is sales revenue?

Gross profit = £150,000 x $\dfrac{40}{100}$ = £60,000

Sales = cost of sales + gross profit, ie £150,000 + £60,000 = **£210,000**

example 2 – calculation of purchases

- Sales are £450,000
- Margin (gross sales margin) is one-fifth
- Opening inventory is £40,000; closing inventory is £50,000

What are purchases?

Gross profit = £450,000 x $\dfrac{1}{5}$ =   £90,000

Cost of sales = sales – gross profit, ie £450,000 – £90,000 = £360,000

The purchases calculation is:

Opening inventory	£40,000
+ Purchases (missing figure)	?
– Closing inventory	£50,000
= Cost of sales	£360,000
Therefore purchases =	**£370,000**

example 3 – calculation of cost of sales and closing inventory

- Sales are £65,000
- Margin (gross sales margin) is 20%
- Opening inventory is £7,500
- Purchases are £46,000

What is:

(a)   cost of sales?

(b)   closing inventory?

(a) £65,000 x $\frac{100 - 20}{100}$ = **£52,000 cost of sales**

(b) Using cost of sales to calculate closing inventory:

Opening inventory	£7,500
+ Purchases	£46,000
– Closing inventory (missing figure)	?
= Cost of sales	£52,000 from (a)

Therefore closing inventory is:

(£7,500 + £46,000) – £52,000   **= £1,500**

Note: the same technique can be used to calculate any one of the figures above, when the amounts are given for the others.

example 4 – calculation of goods for own use or inventory losses

· Sales are £500,000

· Margin is 40%

· Opening inventory is £15,000

· Purchases are £310,000

· Closing inventory is £22,000

What is the amount of goods for own use taken by the owner?

Cost of sales is:

£500,000   x $\frac{100 - 40}{100}$ = £300,000

Opening inventory	£15,000
+ Purchases	£310,000
– Closing inventory	£22,000
	£303,000

With cost of sales of £300,000 (as calculated from sales and gross sales margin), the closing inventory is estimated to be £25,000 (ie, £15,000 + £310,000 – £25,000 = £300,000). However, the actual closing inventory is £22,000 so the goods taken by the owner for own use are:

£25,000 estimated inventory – £22,000 actual inventory = **£3,000 drawings**

Note: as well as calculating goods for own use, this same technique can be used to calculate **inventory losses**, which may occur as a result of an event such as a fire, a flood or a theft.

REASONABLENESS OF FIGURES

When preparing financial statements from calculated figures, it is appropriate to 'step back' and, before using the figure, to ask 'does this seem reasonable?' For example, if gross sales margin was 100% this year compared with 20% last year, it would make sense to question and to double-check the calculation.

There is a need to be aware that, when using a calculated figure, it may differ from an actual balance. For example, using a gross sales margin of 30% assumes that this applies to all goods sold – in most businesses, different percentages will relate to different goods and the 30% is simply an average. Wherever possible, when preparing incomplete records, an actual balance is preferable to a calculated figure.

As with all calculated figures, accounting staff should exercise an element of 'professional scepticism' as to the reasonableness of given figures in a particular context.

Chapter Summary	▪ Incomplete records is the term used where some aspect of the accounting system is missing.
	▪ In order to prepare financial statements, the accountant may well have to calculate.
	– capital at the beginning of the year
	– purchases and sales for the year
	– cash book summary for the year
	– profit for the year
	▪ It is important that accounting staff preparing financial statements act with integrity.
	▪ On the basis of these calculations, the accountant can then construct the financial statements without recourse to a trial balance.
	▪ Two ratios and percentages used in incomplete records accounting are:
	– gross profit mark-up
	– gross profit margin (gross sales margin)

■ The value of inventory losses caused by fire, flood or theft is calculated using margins and mark-ups.

■ When preparing financial statements from incomplete records, accounting staff should:

 – assess whether figures are reasonable

 – note that there may be a difference between an actual balance and a calculation

 – exercise 'professional scepticism' as to the reasonableness of figures

Key Terms

incomplete records	financial records where some aspect of the accounting system is missing
integrity	being straightforward and honest in all professional and business relationships
gross profit mark-up	profit percentage or fraction added to the buying price
gross profit margin (gross sales margin)	profit percentage or fraction based on the selling price
inventory loss	loss of inventory caused by fire, flood or theft
professional scepticism	part of the assessment of the reasonableness of given figures within a particular context

Activities

Blank photocopiable layouts of the statement of profit or loss and the statement of financial position are included in the Appendix – it is advisable to enlarge them up to A4 size.

4.1   •   Cost of sales for the year is £200,000
        •   Mark-up is 30%

What are sales for the year (net of VAT)?

(a)	£140,000	
(b)	£200,000	
(c)	£260,000	
(d)	£300,000	

4.2   •   Sales for the year are £120,000 (including VAT at 20%)
        •   Gross profit margin is one-quarter
        •   Opening inventory is £10,000; closing inventory is £12,000

What are purchases for the year (net of VAT)?

(a)	£25,000	
(b)	£77,000	
(c)	£102,000	
(d)	£125,000	

4.3   You are preparing accounts from incomplete records. Trade receivables at the start of the year were £2,500, and at the end were £3,250. Bank receipts from receivables total £17,850; cash sales total £2,500 (net of VAT). What is the sales revenue figure for the year (net of VAT)?

(a)	£17,850	
(b)	£17,100	
(c)	£18,600	
(d)	£21,100	

4.4   Jane Price owns a fashion shop called 'Trendsetters'. She has been in business for one year and, although she does not keep a full set of accounting records, the following information has been produced for the first year of trading, which ended on 31 December 20-4:

Summary of the business bank account for the year ended 31 December 20-4:

	£
Capital introduced	60,000
Receipts from sales	153,500
Payments to suppliers	95,000
Advertising	4,830
Wages	15,000
Rent and rates	8,750
Administration expenses	5,000
Shop fittings	50,000
Drawings	15,020

Summary of assets and liabilities as at 31 December 20-4:

	£
Shop fittings at cost	50,000
Inventory	73,900
Trade receivables	2,500
Trade payables	65,000

Other information:

- Jane wishes to depreciate the shop fittings at 20% per year using the straight-line method
- At 31 December 20-4, rent is prepaid by £250, and wages of £550 are owing

You are to:

(a)   Calculate the amount of sales during the year.

(b)   Calculate the amount of purchases during the year.

(c)   Calculate the amounts of:

- rent and rates
- wages

to be shown in the statement of profit or loss for the year ended 31 December 20-4.

(d)   Prepare Jane Price's statement of profit or loss for the year ended 31 December 20-4.

(e)   Prepare Jane Price's statement of financial position at 31 December 20-4.

Note: VAT is to be ignored on all transactions.

4.5 James Harvey runs a grocery shop. He has taken goods for his own use from the shop, but has not kept any records. You are to calculate from the accounting records the value of inventory he has taken for his own use. The following information is available:
- sales for the year, £180,000
- opening inventory at the beginning of the year, £21,500
- purchases for the year, £132,000
- closing inventory at the end of the year, £25,000
- the gross profit margin achieved on all sales is 30 per cent

You are to calculate the value of inventory taken during the year by James Harvey for his own use.

Note: VAT is to be ignored on all transactions.

4.6 Colin Smith owns a business which sells specialist central heating parts to trade customers. He has been in business for a number of years. Although he does not keep a full set of accounting records, the following information is available in respect of the year ended 30 June 20-5:

Summary of assets and liabilities:

	1 July 20-4	30 June 20-5
	£	£
Assets		
Inventory	25,000	27,500
Fixtures and fittings (cost £50,000)	40,000	35,000
Trade receivables	36,000	35,000
Bank	1,500	1,210
Liabilities		
Trade payables	32,500	30,000
Accrual: administration expenses	500	700

Summary of the business bank account for the year ended 30 June 20-5:

	£
Administration expenses	30,000
Drawings	28,790
Receipts from trade receivables	121,000
Payments to trade payables	62,500

Other information:
- Fixtures and fittings are being depreciated at 10% per year using the straight line method
- Irrecoverable debts of £550 have been written off during the year

You are to:

(a) Calculate the amount of sales during the year ended 30 June 20-5.

(b) Calculate the amount of purchases during the year ended 30 June 20-5.

(c) Calculate the amount of administration expenses to be shown in the statement of profit or loss for the year ended 30 June 20-5.

(d) Prepare Colin Smith's statement of profit or loss for the year ended 30 June 20-5.

(e) Prepare Colin Smith's statement of financial position at 30 June 20-5.

Note: VAT is to be ignored on all transactions.

4.7 This Activity is about finding missing figures in ledger accounts where the records are incomplete.

You are working on the financial statements of a business for the year ended 31 March 20-9. You have the following information:

Day book summaries for the year	Net £	VAT £	Total £
Sales	168,000	33,600	201,600
Purchases	96,000	19,200	115,200

All sales and purchases are on credit terms.

Balances as at:	31 March 20-8 £	31 March 20-9 £
Trade receivables	20,400	27,100
Trade payables	12,600	11,800

Further information:	Net £	VAT £	Total £
Selling expenses	12,400	2,480	14,880

Selling expenses are not included in the purchases figure in purchases day book.

Bank summary	Dr £		Cr £
Balance b/d	12,460	Travel expenses	2,300
Trade receivables	192,650	Selling expenses	14,880
Interest received	55	Trade payables	112,150
		HMRC for VAT	10,425
		Drawings	21,000
		Wages	33,280
		Balance c/d	11,130
	205,165		205,165

(a) Using the figures given on the previous page, prepare the sales ledger control account for the year ended 31 March 20-9. Show clearly discounts as the balancing figure.

Sales ledger control account

(b) Find the closing balance for VAT by preparing the VAT control account for the year ended 31 March 20-9. Use the figures given on the previous page.

Note: The business is not charged VAT on its travel expenses.

VAT control account

		Balance b/d	3,050

4.8 Peter Kamara runs Clothing Supplies, a small clothing wholesalers. Peter is convinced that various items of clothing have been stolen during the year and he asks you to calculate, from the accounting details, the value of inventory stolen. The following information is available:

- sales for the year, £600,000
- opening inventory at the beginning of the year, £20,000
- purchases for the year, £430,000
- closing inventory at the end of the year, £26,000
- the gross profit margin achieved on all sales is 30 per cent

You are to calculate the value of inventory stolen (if any) during the year.

Note: VAT is to be ignored on all transactions.

5 Sole trader financial statements

this chapter covers...

In this chapter we look at preparing the year end financial statements of sole traders (that is, one person running their own business). We present the financial statements – statement of profit or loss and statement of financial position – using the conventional format.

This chapter shows how the financial statements are adjusted to:

■ *present a more relevant and faithful representation of profit, and assets and liabilities*

■ *enable comparisons to be made with financial statements from previous years*

■ *enable users of financial statements to understand and be assured of the information given*

The chapter continues with conventional format financial statements by bringing together into a trial balance the adjustments for:

■ *closing inventory*

■ *accruals and prepayments*

■ *depreciation of non-current assets*

■ *irrecoverable debts*

■ *allowance for doubtful debts*

We then see how these adjustments are incorporated into the conventional format financial statements.

SOLE TRADERS

As we have seen in Chapter 1, sole traders are people who run their own businesses – shops, factories, farms, garages, local franchises, etc. The businesses are generally small because the owner usually has a limited amount of capital. Profits are often small and, after the owner has taken out drawings, are usually ploughed back into the business.

The financial statements (final accounts) of a sole trader comprise:

■ statement of profit or loss

■ statement of financial position

Such financial statements are produced annually at the end of the financial year (which can end at any date – it doesn't have to be the calendar year). The financial statements can be produced more often in order to give information to the sole trader on how the business is progressing.

drawings, capital injections, profits or losses

The capital account shows the sole trader's stake in the business. It records:

■ opening capital at the start of the year

■ plus capital injections (if any) added during the year

■ plus profit for the year, or minus loss for the year

■ minus drawings taken by the owner during the year

The layout for capital account in the double-entry system is as follows:

Dr		**Capital account**		Cr
	£			£
Statement of profit of loss (loss for the year)			Balance b/d (opening capital)	
Drawings (owner's drawings for the year)			Bank/cash (capital injection)	
Balance c/d (closing capital)			Statement of profit or loss (profit for the year)	

Note that closing capital is the figure shown in the year end statement of financial position.

A completed capital account is shown on page 89.

FINANCIAL STATEMENTS: THE ADJUSTMENTS

Many Activities and Assessments focus on aspects of the preparation of financial statements in the conventional format used by accountants. For example, you may be asked to prepare some, or all, of a statement of profit or loss and statement of financial position. There may be a number of adjustments incorporated into the year end financial statements. The diagram on the next page summarises the year end adjustments and their effect on the financial statements. The adjustments are made in order to:

- present a more relevant and faithful representation of profit, and assets and liabilities

- enable comparisons to be made with financial statements from previous years

- enable users of financial statements to understand and be assured of the information given

The Case Study on page 86 brings together all of these adjustments. Although in total the Case Study is more complex than would be required in an Assessment, it does provide a useful reference point which shows the adjustments incorporated into the financial statements of a sole trader.

The Activities at the end of this chapter are based on the preparation of financial statements from a trial balance and provide practice to help with your studies in preparing conventional format financial statements.

Note that in AAT Assessments:

- you will always be given a balancing trial balance which incorporates the adjustments

- you will be given an outline pro-forma of the financial statements together with a list of pro-forma names to use

- individual components of the trading account and expenses are to be labelled and shown in the appropriate section of the pro-forma

- some adaptation of the pro-forma names may be needed – eg interest paid may need to be shown as finance costs – and some accounts may need to be combined – eg cash + bank = cash and cash equivalents

- some trial balance accounts may need translation to the pro-forma names – eg purchases ledger control accounts to be shown as trade payables

- some account balances could appear on either side of the trial balance – eg VAT, loans, bank – and need to be treated correctly in the financial statement pro-forma

- accounts such as discounts received and interest received should be treated as separate additions to gross profit, rather than being shown as negative expenses

SUMMARY OF YEAR END ADJUSTMENTS FOR FINANCIAL STATEMENTS

ADJUSTMENT	STATEMENT OF PROFIT OR LOSS	STATEMENT OF FINANCIAL POSITION
closing inventory	• deduct from purchases	• current asset
accrual of expenses	• add to expense	• current liability
prepayment of expenses	• deduct from expense	• current asset
accrual of income	• add to income	• current asset
prepayment of income	• deduct from income	• current liability
depreciation charge/ accumulated depreciation of non-current assets	• depreciation charge: expense	• non-current assets reduced by accumulated depreciation to give carrying amount
irrecoverable debts	• expense	• deduct from trade receivables
disposal of non-current asset	• debit balance: expense (loss on disposal) • credit balance: income (gain on disposal)	• non-current assets reduced by disposal
creation of, or increase in, allowance for doubtful debts	• expense	• trade receivables figure reduced by total amount of allowance
decrease in allowance for doubtful debts	• income	• trade receivables figure reduced by total amount of allowance
goods or services taken by the owner for own use	• add to sales revenue	• add to drawings

Note that, in AAT Assessments, you may be required to combine account balances before transferring the net amount or total amount to the statement of profit or loss or statement of financial position. Examples include sales minus sales returns equals net sales, purchases minus purchases returns equals net purchases, trade receivables less allowance for doubtful debts equals net trade receivables. An Assessment will always tell you when such combining is to be done – usually in the form of a statement of the business' policy.

SOLE TRADER FINANCIAL STATEMENTS

situation

You are the accountant to Olivia Boulton, a sole trader, who runs a kitchen and cookware shop. Her bookkeeper extracted the year end trial balance and you have incorporated into it the adjustments advised to you by Olivia Boulton. The adjusted trial balance is as follows:

Trial balance of Olivia Boulton as at 31 December 20-2

	Dr £	Cr £
Opening inventory	50,000	
Purchases	420,000	
Sales revenue		557,500
Closing inventory	42,000	42,000
Shop expenses	6,200	
Shop wages	33,300	
Prepayment of shop wages	200	
Telephone expenses	600	
Accrual of telephone expenses		100
Interest paid	8,000	
Travel expenses	550	
Discounts allowed	450	
Discounts received		900
Disposal of non-current asset		250
Premises at cost	250,000	
Shop fittings at cost	40,000	
Premises: depreciation charge	5,000	
Shop fittings: depreciation charge	6,400	
Premises: accumulated depreciation		15,000
Shop fittings: accumulated depreciation		14,400
Sales ledger control	10,000	
Irrecoverable debts	500	
Allowance for doubtful debts		250
Allowance for doubtful debts: adjustment	50	
Purchases ledger control		11,250
Bank	2,650	
Capital		125,000
Drawings	24,000	
Loan from bank (repayable in 20-9)		130,000
Value Added Tax		3,250
	899,900	899,900

You are to prepare the financial statements of Olivia Boulton for the year ended 31 December 20-2, using the conventional format.

solution

The financial statements incorporating these adjustments are shown on the next two pages. A summary of the effect of each adjustment is given below.

closing inventory

- deduct £42,000 from purchases in the statement of profit or loss
- show inventory at £42,000 as a current asset in the statement of financial position

prepayment of expenses

- show £200 prepayment of shop wages as a current asset in the statement of financial position

accrual of expenses

- show £100 accrual of telephone expenses as a current liability in the statement of financial position

depreciation of non-current assets

- in the statement of profit or loss show as expenses the depreciation charges for premises £5,000 and shop fittings £6,400
- in the statement of financial position show accumulated depreciation amounts deducted from non-current assets to give carrying amounts as follows:

	Cost	Accumulated depreciation	Carrying amount
	£	£	£
Premises	250,000	15,000	235,000
Shop fittings	40,000	14,400	25,600
	290,000	29,400	260,600

disposal of non-current asset

During the year a non-current asset has been sold. The bookkeeping entries for disposals have been made and all that remains is a credit balance of £250 on disposals account. This amount is shown as income, being a gain on disposal, in the statement of profit or loss. (A debit balance on disposals account would mean a loss on disposal – this would be shown as an expense in the statement of profit or loss.)

irrecoverable debts

- record irrecoverable debts of £500 as an expense in the statement of profit or loss

allowance for doubtful debts: adjustment

- in the statement of profit or loss record the £50 amount of the increase (debit side of trial balance) in allowance for doubtful debts as an expense
- in the statement of financial position deduct £250 from the trade receivables figure of £10,000 to give net receivables of £9,750 – it is this amount that is listed in current assets

Note that, where there is a reduction in the allowance for doubtful debts, show the amount of the reduction as income in the statement of profit or loss.

financial statements

The financial statements of Olivia Boulton that you prepare are shown below.

OLIVIA BOULTON STATEMENT OF PROFIT OR LOSS for the year ended 31 December 20-2		
	£	£
Sales revenue		557,500
Opening inventory	50,000	
Purchases	420,000	
	470,000	
Less Closing inventory	42,000	
Cost of sales		428,000
Gross profit		129,500
Add other income:		
Discounts received		900
Gain on disposal of non-current asset		250
		130,650
Less expenses:		
Shop expenses	6,200	
Shop wages	33,300	
Telephone	600	
Finance costs (interest paid)	8,000	
Travel expenses	550	
Discounts allowed	450	
Depreciation charges: premises	5,000	
shop fittings	6,400	
Irrecoverable debts	500	
Allowance for doubtful debts: adjustment	50	
		61,050
Profit for the year		69,600

Note that the balances of accounts such as discounts received, interest received, commission received, gain on disposal of non-current asset etc are always listed in the statement of profit or loss under the heading of **other income** and are added to the gross profit.

STATEMENT OF FINANCIAL POSITION
as at 31 December 20-2

Non-current assets	Cost	Accumulated depreciation	Carrying amount
	£	£	£
Premises	250,000	15,000	235,000
Shop fittings	40,000	14,400	25,600
	290,000	29,400	260,600
Current assets			
Inventory		42,000	
Trade receivables	10,000		
Less allowance for doubtful debts	250		
		9,750	
Prepayment of expenses		200	
Cash and cash equivalents (Bank)		2,650	
Total current assets		54,600	
Current liabilities			
Trade payables	11,250		
Accrual of expenses	100		
Value Added Tax	3,250		
Total current liabilities		14,600	
Net current assets			40,000
			300,600
Non-current liabilities			
Loan from bank			130,000
Net assets			170,600
Financed by:			
Capital*			
Opening capital			125,000
Add Profit for the year			69,600
			194,600
Less Drawings			24,000
Closing capital			170,600

Note: non-current liabilities, eg long-term loans, are shown in the statement of financial position as a deduction from the assets of the business

*The capital account of Olivia Boulton in the double entry system is as follows:

Dr			Capital account		Cr
20-2		£	20-2		£
31 Dec	Drawings	24,000	1 Jan	Balance b/d	125,000
31 Dec	Balance c/d	170,600	31 Dec	Statement of profit or loss	69,600
		194,600			194,600
20-3			20-3		
			1 Jan	Balance b/d	170,600

Note: there was no capital injection added during the year.

THE USE OF COST OF SALES ACCOUNT

In some trial balances there is a debit column balance given for cost of sales (also referred to as cost of goods sold). This happens because the cost of sales calculation has been done already, and no amounts are shown in the trial balance for:

■ in the debit column

- opening inventory

- purchases

■ in the credit column

- purchases returns (if any)

- closing inventory (but the debit column balance for closing inventory is still shown, as this is the amount which is an asset for the statement of financial position)

The calculation for cost of sales (cost of goods sold) is:

	Opening inventory
plus	Purchases
less	Purchases returns (if any)
less	Closing inventory
equals	Cost of sales

It is the final figure for cost of sales that is shown in the debit column of the trial balance – the other amounts are not shown – when the business is using a cost of sales account.

cost of sales account

This account brings together the amounts that make up cost of sales, as follows (using the figures from Olivia Boulton's trial balance on page 86):

Dr			Cost of sales account		Cr
20-2		£	20-2		£
31 Dec	Opening inventory	50,000	31 Dec	Purchases returns*	–
31 Dec	Purchases	420,000	31 Dec	Closing inventory	42,000
			31 Dec	Balance c/d	428,000
		470,000			470,000
31 Dec	Balance b/d	428,000	31 Dec	Statement of profit or loss	428,000

* **Note:** there were no purchases returns in Olivia Boulton's trial balance

The balance of the cost of sales account, £428,000, is transferred to the statement of profit or loss where it is deducted from sales to give gross profit:

OLIVIA BOULTON
STATEMENT OF PROFIT OR LOSS (extract)
for the year ended 31 December 20-2

	£	£
Sales revenue (less sales returns, if any)		557,500
Less Cost of sales		428,000
Gross profit		129,500

As you see, this is the same gross profit as we have seen already on page 88, but here gross profit has been calculated in just three lines (although there may be sales returns to deduct from sales revenue). The rest of the statement of profit or loss continues as we have seen previously.

summary

In Activities and Assessments you should be ready for a trial balance to present you with two different circumstances:

either

■ full cost of sales amounts

- opening inventory, in debit column

- purchases, in debit column

- purchases returns (if any), in credit column

- closing inventory, in both debit and credit columns (remember that the debit amount is an asset on the statement of financial position, while the credit amount is used in cost of sales)

or

■ cost of sales account

- cost of sales, in debit column

- closing inventory, in debit column (an asset on the statement of financial position)

In the first circumstance you will need to calculate the figure for cost of sales on the face of the statement of profit or loss. In the second circumstance it is only necessary to deduct cost of sales from the figure for sales (allowing for sales returns, if any) in order to calculate the gross profit figure – after gross profit, the statement of profit or loss continues as we have seen previously.

■   Sole traders are people who run their own businesses; generally their businesses are small because the owner usually has a limited amount of capital.

■   The financial statements of a sole trader comprise:

–   statement of profit or loss
–   statement of financial position

■   Adjustments are made to financial statements in order to improve their relevance and faithful representation.

■   A fully adjusted trial balance incorporates the adjustments for:
–   closing inventory
–   accruals and prepayments
–   depreciation of non-current assets
–   irrecoverable debts
–   allowance for doubtful debts

■   A cost of sales account enables the statement of profit or loss to show gross profit in three lines:

sales revenue, less sales returns (if any)
–   cost of sales
=   gross profit

sole trader   one person running their own business

adjusted trial balance   trial balance which incorporates the accounting adjustments and from which financial statements can be prepared

cost of sales account   account which brings together amounts that make up cost of sales:

opening inventory
+   purchases
–   purchases returns (if any)
–   closing inventory
=   cost of sales

Activities

> Blank photocopiable layouts of the statement of profit or loss and the statement of financial position are included in the Appendix – it is advisable to enlarge them up to A4 size.

5.1 A statement of profit or loss shows a profit for the year of £10,500. It is discovered that no allowance has been made for wages prepaid of £250 and administration expenses accrued of £100 at the year end. What is the adjusted profit for the year?

(a)	£10,150	
(b)	£10,350	
(c)	£10,650	
(d)	£10,850	

5.2 A year end trial balance includes the following amounts:

opening inventory	£5,500
closing inventory	£6,500
purchases	£25,000
sales revenue	£48,000
purchases returns	£1,000
sales returns	£2,000

What is the cost of sales figure for the year?

(a)	£23,000	
(b)	£25,000	
(c)	£26,000	
(d)	£47,000	

5.3 A statement of profit or loss shows a profit for the year of £15,750. The owner of the business wishes to reduce the allowance for doubtful debts by £500 and to write off irrecoverable debts of £300. What is the adjusted profit for the year?

(a) £14,950	
(b) £15,550	
(c) £15,950	
(d) £16,550	

5.4 You have the following trial balance for a sole trader known as Zelah Trading. All the necessary year end adjustments have been made.

(a) Prepare a statement of profit or loss (on the next page) for the business for the year ended 31 March 20-4.

Zelah Trading Trial balance as at 31 March 20-4	Dr £	Cr £
Accruals		950
Bank	3,220	
Capital		22,000
Closing inventory	6,500	6,500
Depreciation charge	3,400	
Discounts allowed	750	
Drawings	6,500	
General expenses	21,240	
Machinery at cost	24,200	
Machinery: accumulated depreciation		8,400
Opening inventory	4,850	
Prepayments	650	
Purchases	85,260	
Purchases ledger control		11,360
Rent	8,900	
Sales revenue		155,210
Sales ledger control	15,350	
Selling expenses	27,890	
Value Added Tax		4,290
	208,710	208,710

Zelah Trading **Statement of profit or loss for the year ended 31 March 20-4**		
	£	£
Sales revenue		
Cost of sales		
Gross profit		
Less expenses:		
Total expenses		
Profit for the year		

(b) Indicate where closing inventory should be shown in the statement of financial position. Tick **one** from:

(a)	As a non-current asset	
(b)	As a current asset	
(c)	As a current liability	
(d)	As a deduction from capital	

(c) State the meaning of a credit balance for Value Added Tax in a trial balance. Tick **one** from:

(a)	HM Revenue & Customs owes the business	
(b)	HM Revenue & Customs is a receivable of the business	
(c)	There is an error – VAT is always a debit balance	
(d)	The business owes HM Revenue & Customs	

5.5   The following adjusted trial balance has been taken from the books of Helena Ostrowska, who sells soft furnishings, as at 31 March 20-5:

	Dr	Cr
	£	£
Sales ledger control	46,280	
Purchases ledger control		24,930
Value Added Tax		3,860
Bank	10,180	
Capital		62,000
Sales revenue		243,820
Purchases	140,950	
Opening inventory	30,030	
Shop wages	40,270	
Accrual of shop wages		940
Heat and light	3,470	
Prepayment of heat and light	220	
Rent and rates	12,045	
Shop fittings at cost	30,000	
Shop fittings: depreciation charge	5,000	
Shop fittings: accumulated depreciation		15,000
Disposal of non-current asset	850	
Irrecoverable debts	200	
Drawings	31,055	
Closing inventory	34,080	34,080
	384,630	384,630

You are to prepare the financial statements of Helena Ostrowska for the year ended 31 March 20-5, using the conventional format.

5.6   The following adjusted trial balance has been taken from the books of Mark Pelisi, a landscape gardener, as at 31 March 20-7:

	Dr £	Cr £
Sales revenue		100,330
Sales returns	120	
Cost of sales	35,710	
Discounts allowed and received	170	240
Drawings	30,090	
Vehicles at cost	24,000	
Vehicles: depreciation charge	6,000	
Vehicles: accumulated depreciation		12,500
Equipment at cost	18,500	
Equipment: depreciation charge	3,500	
Equipment: accumulated depreciation		8,000
Disposal of non-current asset		160
Wages	24,110	
Accrual of wages		400
Advertising	770	
Administration expenses	14,830	
Bank	3,800	
Sales ledger control	3,480	
Irrecoverable debts	350	
Allowance for doubtful debts		620
Allowance for doubtful debts: adjustment		180
Purchases ledger control		2,760
Value Added Tax		1,840
Capital		35,040
Bank loan (repayable in 20-9)		9,000
Closing inventory	5,640	
	171,070	171,070

You are to prepare the financial statements of Mark Pelisi for the year ended 31 March 20-7, using the conventional format.

6 Partnership financial statements

this chapter covers...

So far, when discussing financial statements, we have considered the accounts of a sole trader, ie one person in business. However, a partnership is a common form of business unit, and can be found in the form of:

■ sole traders who have joined together with others in order to raise finance and expand the business

■ family businesses, such as builders, car repairers, gardeners

■ professional businesses such as solicitors, accountants, doctors, dentists

In this chapter we look at

■ the definition of a partnership

■ the accounting requirements of the Partnership Act 1890

■ the accounting requirements which may be incorporated into a partnership agreement

■ the use of capital accounts and current accounts

■ the appropriation of profits

■ the layout of the capital section of the statement of financial position

■ partnership financial statements, using the extended trial balance method and the conventional format

Note: this chapter covers the financial statements of the partnerships that are not limited liability partnerships. LLP financial statements are very similar to those of limited companies – see Chapter 8.

WHAT DOES A PARTNERSHIP INVOLVE?

The Partnership Act of 1890 defines a partnership as:

the relation which subsists between persons carrying on a business in common with a view of profit

As we have seen in Chapter 1, normally, partnerships consist of between two and twenty partners – exceptions being large professional businesses, eg solicitors and accountants, which are often set up as limited liability partnerships (LLPs) under the terms of the Limited Liability Partnership Act, 2000.

Partnerships are often larger businesses than sole traders because, as there is more than one owner, there is likely to be more capital. A partnership may be formed to set up a new business or it may be the logical growth of a sole trader taking in partners to increase the capital.

accounting requirements of a partnership

The accounting requirements of a partnership are:

- either to follow the rules set out in the Partnership Act 1890

- or – and more likely – for the partners to agree amongst themselves, by means of a partnership agreement (see page 101), to follow different accounting rules

Unless the partners agree otherwise, the Partnership Act 1890 states the following accounting rules:

- profits and losses are to be shared equally between the partners

- no partner is entitled to a salary

- partners are not entitled to receive interest on their capital

- interest is not to be charged on partners' drawings

- when a partner contributes more capital than agreed, he or she is entitled to receive interest at five per cent per annum on the excess

Note: for AAT Assessments you should be aware of the existence and purpose of the Partnership Act, but you do not need to be able to recall the provisions of the Act.

As mentioned above, the partners may well decide to follow different accounting rules – these will be set out in a partnership agreement, and, in AAT Assessments, relevant details of the partnership will be given.

FINANCIAL STATEMENTS OF A PARTNERSHIP

A partnership prepares the same type of year end financial statements as a sole trader business:

■ statement of profit or loss
■ statement of financial position

The main difference is that, immediately after the statement of profit or loss, follows a **partnership appropriation account.** The purpose of this is to show how the profit or loss from the statement of profit or loss is shared amongst the partners. Note that, in AAT Assessments, a pro-forma partnership appropriation account will be given when required.

example of sharing profits and losses

Jan, Kay and Lil are partners sharing profits and losses equally; their statement of profit or loss for 20-1 shows a profit of £60,000. The appropriation of profits appears as:

JAN, KAY AND LIL PARTNERSHIP APPROPRIATION ACCOUNT for the year ended 31 December 20-1	£
Profit for the year	60,000
Profit share:	
Jan	20,000
Kay	20,000
Lil	20,000
	60,000

The above is a simple appropriation of profits. A more complex appropriation account (see Case Study on page 103) deals with other accounting points from the partnership agreement.

Note that a loss for the year will be allocated to partners in a similar way.

PARTNERSHIP AGREEMENT

The accounting rules from the Partnership Act are often varied with the agreement of all partners, by means of a partnership agreement. In particular, a partnership agreement – which may not always be a formal document – will usually cover the following main points:

- division of profits and losses between partners (which may be expressed as a ratio, fraction or percentage)
- partners' salaries/commission
- whether interest is to be allowed on partners' capital, and at what rate
- whether interest is to be charged on partners' drawings, and at what rate

The money amounts involved for each of these points (where allowed by the partnership agreement) are shown in the partnership appropriation account (see Case Study on page 103).

division of profits and losses between partners

The Partnership Act states that, in the absence of an agreement to the contrary, profits and losses are to be shared equally. A partner's share of the profits is normally taken out of the business in the form of drawings. Clearly, if one partner has contributed much more capital than the other partner(s), it would be unfair to apply this clause from the Act. Consequently, many partnerships agree to share profits and losses on a different basis – often in the same proportions as they have contributed capital. Note that, in Activities and Assessments, you will normally be told the agreed division of profits and losses; however, if there is no mention of this, you should assume that the partners receive an equal share.

partners' salaries/commission

Although the Act says that no partner is entitled to a salary, it is quite usual in the partnership agreement for one or more partners to be paid a salary. The reason for doing this is that often in a partnership, one of the partners spends more time working in the partnership than the other(s). The agreement to pay a salary is in recognition of the work done. Note that partners' salaries are not shown as an expense in the statement of profit or loss; instead they are recorded in the partnership appropriation account.

Many professional partnerships, such as solicitors and accountants, have junior partners who receive a partnership salary because they work full-time in the business, but have not yet contributed any capital. In a partnership, there may not be a requirement to contribute capital, unless the partnership agreement states otherwise; however, most partners will eventually do so.

As an alternative – or in addition – to a salary, a partner might be paid a commission – for example on sales. As with a salary, this is not shown as an expense in the statement of profit or loss but, instead, is recorded in the partnership appropriation account.

interest allowed on capital

Many partnerships include a clause in their partnership agreement which allows interest to be paid on capital; the rate of interest will be stated also. This clause is used to compensate partners for the loss of use of their capital, ie it is not available to invest elsewhere. Often, interest is allowed on capital in partnerships where profits and losses are shared equally – it is one way of partly adjusting for different capital balances. As noted earlier, the Partnership Act does not permit interest to be paid on capital, so reference to it must be made in the partnership agreement.

Note that Activities and AAT Assessments will state the amount of interest allowed on partners' capital – you will not need to calculate it.

interest charged on partners' drawings

In order to discourage partners from drawing out too much money from the business early in the financial year, the partnership agreement may stipulate that interest is to be charged on partners' drawings, and at what rate. This acts as a penalty against early withdrawal in the year when the business may be short of cash.

The amount of interest charged on drawings for the year is shown in the partnership appropriation account, where it increases the profit to be shared amongst the partners.

Note that Activities and AAT Assessments will state the amount of interest charged on partners' drawings – you will not need to calculate it.

NATURE AND CONTENT OF PARTNERS' CAPITAL ACCOUNTS AND CURRENT ACCOUNTS

The important bookkeeping difference between a sole trader and a partnership is that each partner usually has a capital account **and** a current account. The capital account is normally **fixed**, and only alters if a permanent capital increase (credit partner's capital account) or decrease (debit partner's capital account) takes place. The current account is **fluctuating** and it is to this account that:

- share of profit is credited
- share of loss is debited
- salary is credited
- interest allowed on partners' capital is credited
- interest charged on partners' drawings is debited
- drawings and goods for own use are debited

Thus, the current account is treated as a **working** account, while capital account remains fixed, except for capital introduced or withdrawn – usually done by payments into the bank account for capital introduced, or payments out of the bank account for capital withdrawn.

A partner's current account has the following layout:

Dr	Partner Aye: current account	Cr
	£	£
Drawings/goods for own use	Balance b/d	
Interest charged on drawings*	Salary*	
Loss share	Interest on capital*	
Balance c/d	Profit share	

*if these items are allowed by the partnership agreement

Note that whilst the normal balance on a partner's current account is credit, when the partner has drawn out more than his or her share of the profits, then the balance will be debit.

Case Study

ALI AND BOB:
APPROPRIATION OF PARTNERSHIP PROFITS

As we have seen earlier in this chapter, the appropriation account follows the statement of profit or loss and shows how profit for the year has been divided amongst the partners. This Case Study shows a partnership salary (which is not shown as an expense in the statement of profit or loss), interest allowed on partners' capital, and interest charged on partners' drawings.

situation

Ali and Bob are in partnership sharing profits and losses 60 per cent and 40 per cent respectively. Profit for the year ended 31 March 20-4 is £42,000.

At 1 April 20-3 (the start of the year), the partners have the following balances:

	Capital account	Current account
	£	£
Ali	40,000	2,000 Cr
Bob	30,000	400 Cr

- there have been no changes to the capital accounts during the year; interest is allowed on partners' capitals at the rate of eight per cent per year
- Bob is entitled to a salary of £16,000 per year
- during the year partners' drawings were: Ali £18,000, Bob £24,000
- interest charged on partners' drawings for the year was: Ali £900, Bob £1,200

solution

The appropriation of profits will be made as follows:

ALI AND BOB
PARTNERSHIP APPROPRIATION ACCOUNT
for the year ended 31 March 20-4

	£	£
Profit for the year		42,000
Add interest charged on partners' drawings:		
Ali	900	
Bob	1,200	2,100
		44,100
Less appropriation of profit:		
Salary: Bob		16,000
Interest allowed on partners' capitals:		
Ali £40,000 x 8%	3,200	
Bob £30,000 x 8%	2,400	5,600
Profit available for distribution		22,500
Profit share:		
Ali (60%)	13,500	
Bob (40%)	9,000	
Total profit distributed		22,500

Note that all of the available profit – after allowing for interest charged on drawings, salary, and interest allowed on capital – is shared amongst the partners, in the ratio in which they share profits and losses.

The partners' current accounts for the year are shown on the next page. Note that the layout for the partners' current accounts uses a normal 'T' account but in a side-by-side format with a column for each partner on both the debit and credit sides. As an alternative, separate current accounts can be produced for each partner.

Dr		Ali	Bob		**Partners' current accounts**		Ali	Cr Bob
		£	£				£	£
20-3/4				20-3/4				
31 Mar	Drawings	18,000	24,000	1 Apr	Balances b/d		2,000	400
31 Mar	Interest on drawings	900	1,200		Salary		–	16,000
31 Mar	Balance c/d	–	2,600	31 Mar	Interest on capital		3,200	2,400
				31 Mar	Profit share		13,500	9,000
				31 Mar	Balance c/d		200	–
		18,900	27,800				18,900	27,800
20-4/5				20-4/5				
1 Apr	Balance b/d	200	–	1 Apr	Balance b/d		–	2,600

From the current accounts we can see that Ali has drawn more out than the balance of the account; accordingly, at the end of the year, Ali has a debit balance of £200 on current account. By contrast, Bob has a credit balance of £2,600 on current account.

STATEMENT OF FINANCIAL POSITION

The statement of financial position of a partnership must show the year end balances on each partner's capital and current account. However, the transactions that have taken place on each account can be shown in summary form – in the same way that, in a sole trader's statement of financial position, profit for the year is added and losses and drawings for the year are deducted.

The other sections of the statement of financial position – non-current assets, current assets, current and long-term liabilities – are presented in the same way as for a sole trader.

The following is an example statement of financial position layout for the 'financed by' section (the other sections of the statement of financial position are not shown). It details the capital and current accounts of the partnership of Ali and Bob (see Case Study above).

ALI AND BOB, IN PARTNERSHIP			
STATEMENT OF FINANCIAL POSITION (EXTRACT) as at 31 March 20-4			
FINANCED BY	Ali	Bob	Total
	£	£	£
Capital accounts	40,000	30,000	70,000
Current accounts	(200)	2,600	2,400
	39,800	32,600	72,400

PARTNERSHIP FINANCIAL STATEMENTS FROM THE TRIAL BALANCE

Financial statements for a partnership can be prepared using the extended trial balance method and can then be set out in the conventional format. The procedures are exactly the same as for sole traders. The only differences to note are that partners' capital and current accounts are shown in the statement of financial position. Transactions affecting the partners' current accounts – share of profits, partners' salaries, interest allowed on capital, interest charged on drawings, drawings, etc – can be shown either in the form of a double-entry 'T' account (see previous page for an example), or directly on the face of the statement of financial position (see the following Case Study). Whichever is done, it is the closing balances of the capital and current accounts – shown separately for each partner – that are added in to the 'financed by' section of the statement of financial position.

Case Study

RAMJIT SINGH AND VETA BIX: PARTNERSHIP FINANCIAL STATEMENTS

situation

The extended trial balance for the partnership of Ramjit Singh and Veta Bix, trading as 'RaVe Music', at 31 December 20-5 is shown on the next page. All columns of the ETB have been completed ready for preparation of financial statements in the conventional format.

Note that the ETB includes the following points:

- there are both accruals and prepayments
- non-current assets have been depreciated
- during the year the partners have taken goods for their own use – purchases have been decreased and the goods charged to each partner (note that the amounts of goods for own use have been shown separately on the ETB to show clearly the accounting treatment; they can be incorporated into the figure for drawings)
- one partner, Veta Bix, receives a salary* – this is shown in the statement of profit or loss columns and the statement of financial position columns
- interest has been allowed on partners' capital accounts*: £5,000 for Ramjit Singh and £4,500 for Veta Bix – shown in the statement of profit or loss and the statement of financial position columns
- the partners share remaining profits* equally – shown in the statement of profit or loss columns and the statement of financial position columns

    * in conventional format financial statements these items are shown in the partnership appropriation account, ie *after* profit for the year has been calculated – see page 108

solution

The financial statements of the partnership of Ramjit Singh and Veta Bix, trading as 'RaVe Music', are shown in ETB format on the next page and in the conventional format on pages 108 and 109.

EXTENDED TRIAL BALANCE   RAMJIT SINGH AND VETA BIX, IN PARTNERSHIP, TRADING AS 'RAVE MUSIC'   31 DECEMBER 20-5

Account name	Ledger balances		Adjustments		Statement of profit or loss		Statement of financial position	
	Dr £	Cr £	Dr £	Cr £	Dr £	Cr £	Dr £	Cr £
Opening inventory	20,000				20,000			
Sales revenue		250,000				250,000		
Purchases	120,000			900	119,100			
Premises at cost	200,000						200,000	
Premises: accumulated depreciation		9,000		3,000				12,000
Fixtures and fittings at cost	20,000						20,000	
Fixtures and fittings: accumulated depreciation		8,000		2,000				10,000
Wages and salaries	35,000		1,700		36,700			
Shop expenses	20,000			800	19,200			
Sales ledger control	3,000						3,000	
Purchases ledger control		7,000						7,000
Value Added Tax		4,000						4,000
Bank		2,000						2,000
Bank loan		80,000						80,000
Capital account: Ramjit Singh		50,000						50,000
Capital account: Veta Bix		45,000						45,000
Current account: Ramjit Singh		4,000						4,000
Current account: Veta Bix		1,000						1,000
Drawings: Ramjit Singh	24,000						24,000	
Drawings: Veta Bix	18,000						18,000	
Goods for own use: Ramjit Singh			500				500	
Goods for own use: Veta Bix			400				400	
Closing inventory: statement of profit or loss			30,000			30,000		
Closing inventory: statement of financial position			30,000				30,000	
Accruals				1,700				1,700
Prepayments			800				800	
Depreciation charge			5,000		5,000			
Partnership salary: Veta Bix					10,000			10,000
Interest on capital: Ramjit Singh					5,000			5,000
Interest on capital: Veta Bix					4,500			4,500
Profit/loss: Ramjit Singh					30,250			30,250
Profit/loss: Veta Bix					30,250			30,250
	460,000	460,000	38,400	38,400	280,000	280,000	296,700	296,700

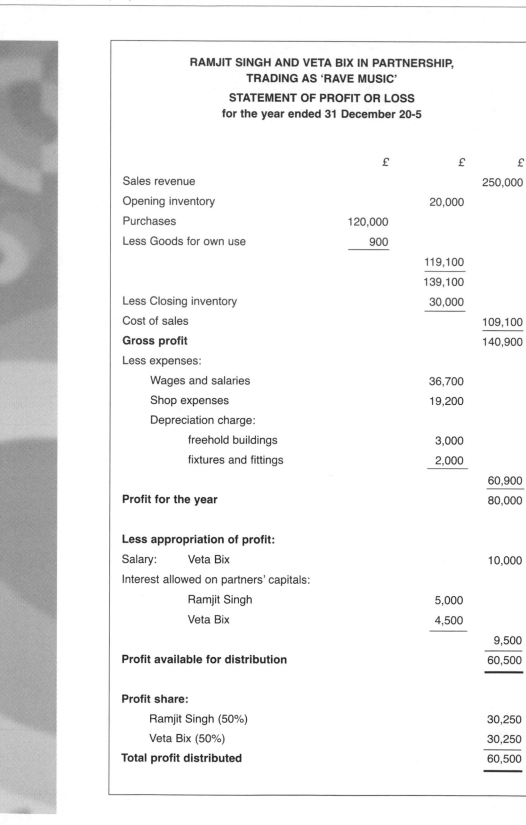

**RAMJIT SINGH AND VETA BIX IN PARTNERSHIP,
TRADING AS 'RAVE MUSIC'**
STATEMENT OF PROFIT OR LOSS
for the year ended 31 December 20-5

	£	£	£
Sales revenue			250,000
Opening inventory		20,000	
Purchases	120,000		
Less Goods for own use	900		
		119,100	
		139,100	
Less Closing inventory		30,000	
Cost of sales			109,100
Gross profit			140,900
Less expenses:			
Wages and salaries		36,700	
Shop expenses		19,200	
Depreciation charge:			
freehold buildings		3,000	
fixtures and fittings		2,000	
			60,900
Profit for the year			80,000
Less appropriation of profit:			
Salary:　　Veta Bix			10,000
Interest allowed on partners' capitals:			
Ramjit Singh		5,000	
Veta Bix		4,500	
			9,500
Profit available for distribution			60,500
Profit share:			
Ramjit Singh (50%)			30,250
Veta Bix (50%)			30,250
Total profit distributed			60,500

**RAMJIT SINGH AND VETA BIX IN PARTNERSHIP,
TRADING AS 'RAVE MUSIC'**

STATEMENT OF FINANCIAL POSITION as at 31 December 20-5

Non-current assets	Cost	Accumulated depreciation	Carrying amount
	£	£	£
Premises	200,000	12,000	188,000
Fixtures and fittings	20,000	10,000	10,000
	220,000	22,000	198,000
Current assets			
Inventory (closing)		30,000	
Trade receivables		3,000	
Prepayments		800	
Total current assets		33,800	
Current liabilities			
Trade payables	7,000		
Value Added Tax	4,000		
Accruals	1,700		
Cash and cash equivalents (Bank)	2,000		
Total current liabilities		14,700	
Net current assets			19,100
			217,100
Non-current liabilities			
Bank loan			80,000
Net assets			137,100

Financed by:

	Ramjit Singh	Veta Bix	
	£	£	£
Capital accounts	50,000	45,000	95,000
Current accounts			
Opening balance	4,000	1,000	
Add: salary	–	10,000	
interest on capital	5,000	4,500	
profit share	30,250	30,250	
	39,250	45,750	
Less: drawings	24,000	18,000	
goods for own use*	500	400	
	14,750	27,350	42,100
			137,100

* goods for own use can be incorporated into the amount for drawings – shown
here separately so that the accounting treatment can be seen clearly.

PREPARING PARTNERSHIP FINANCIAL STATEMENTS

When partnership financial statements are being prepared, the accounts assistant must take note of:

■ the terms of the partnership agreement

■ the policies, regulations, procedures and timescales of the partnership

If there are any discrepancies, unusual features or queries, they should be identified and, where possible, resolved by the accounts assistant. Any outstanding issues will need to be referred to the appropriate person – such as the accounts supervisor, the manager of the partnership, or one or more of the partners.

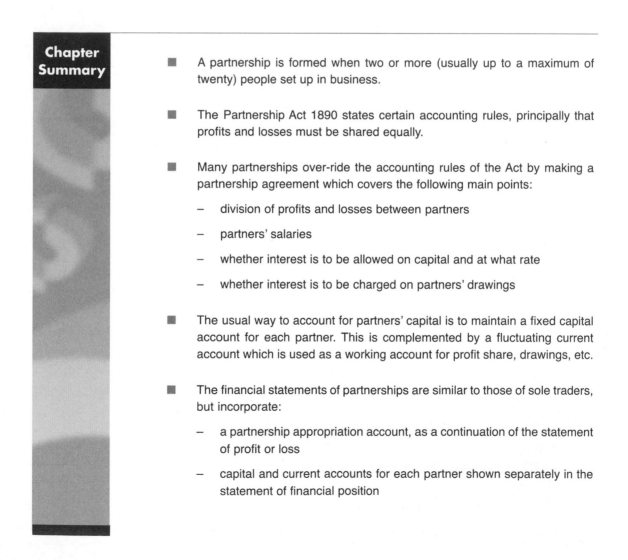

Chapter Summary

■ A partnership is formed when two or more (usually up to a maximum of twenty) people set up in business.

■ The Partnership Act 1890 states certain accounting rules, principally that profits and losses must be shared equally.

■ Many partnerships over-ride the accounting rules of the Act by making a partnership agreement which covers the following main points:

– division of profits and losses between partners

– partners' salaries

– whether interest is to be allowed on capital and at what rate

– whether interest is to be charged on partners' drawings

■ The usual way to account for partners' capital is to maintain a fixed capital account for each partner. This is complemented by a fluctuating current account which is used as a working account for profit share, drawings, etc.

■ The financial statements of partnerships are similar to those of sole traders, but incorporate:

– a partnership appropriation account, as a continuation of the statement of profit or loss

– capital and current accounts for each partner shown separately in the statement of financial position

Key Terms		
	partnership	the relation which subsists between persons carrying on a business in common with a view of profit
	Partnership Act 1890	legislation which includes the accounting rules of partnerships
	partnership agreement	an agreement – which may be informal – between the partners which, amongst other things, often varies the accounting rules of the Partnership Act 1890
	partnership appropriation account	part of the statement of profit or loss which shows how the profit is shared amongst the partners
	capital account	account which records the amount of capital contributed by a partner; usually for a fixed amount, which only alters where a permanent increase or decrease takes place
	current account	a fluctuating account to which is credited: profit share, salary, interest on capital, and to which is debited: loss share, interest on drawings, and drawings

Activities

6.1   In the absence of a partnership agreement, which **one** of the following contravenes the provisions of the Partnership Act 1890?

(a)	No partner is entitled to a salary	
(b)	Profits and losses are to be shared in proportion to capital	
(c)	Partners are not entitled to receive interest on their capital	
(d)	Interest is not to be charged on partners' drawings	

6.2   The current account of a partner, Tara Shah, has a balance at the beginning of the financial year of £550 debit. During the year, the following transactions pass through her current account:

- interest on capital, £900
- salary, £10,000
- drawings, £14,000
- profit share, £4,230

What is the balance of Tara Shah's current account at the end of the financial year?

(a)	£580 Cr	
(b)	£1,220 Dr	
(c)	£1,680 Dr	
(d)	£120 Cr	

6.3   Jan and Lyn are in partnership sharing profits and losses 60% and 40% respectively. At the beginning of the financial year the balances of their current accounts were £6,200 credit and £2,850 credit respectively. During the year the partners took drawings of £1,500 and £1,600 respectively; there were no other current account transactions.

At the end of the year the partnership profit or loss account recorded a loss before appropriation of £7,000.

What is the balance of each partner's current account at the end of the financial year?

(a)	Jan £500 debit; Lyn £1,550 credit	
(b)	Jan £600 credit; Lyn £500 debit	
(c)	Jan £500 credit; Lyn £1,550 debit	
(d)	Jan £600 credit; Lyn £1,650 debit	

6.4 Lysa and Mark are in partnership and own a shop, 'Trends', which sells fashionable teenage clothes. The following figures are extracted from their accounts for the year ended 31 December 20-8:

	£	
Capital accounts at 1 January 2008:		
Lysa	50,000	Cr
Mark	40,000	Cr
Current accounts at 1 January 20-8:		
Lysa	420	Cr
Mark	1,780	Cr
Drawings:		
Lysa	13,000	
Mark	12,250	
Interest charged on drawings:		
Lysa	300	
Mark	250	
Interest allowed on capital:		
Lysa	2,500	
Mark	2,000	
Profit share:		
Lysa	9,300	
Mark	9,300	

Note: neither partner is entitled to receive a salary.

You are to show the partners' capital and current accounts for the year ended 31 December 20-8.

6.5   John James and Steven Hill are in partnership and own a wine shop called 'Grapes'. The following
trial balance has been taken from their accounts for the year ended 31 December 20-5:

	Dr £	Cr £
Capital accounts:		
James		38,000
Hill		32,000
Current accounts:		
James	3,000	
Hill		1,000
Drawings:		
James	10,000	
Hill	22,000	
Sales revenue		174,000
Cost of sales	85,000	
Rent and rates	7,500	
Advertising	12,000	
Heat and light	3,500	
Wages and salaries	18,000	
Sundry expenses	4,000	
Shop fittings at cost	20,000	
*Closing inventory – statement of financial position	35,000	
Bank	29,000	
Sales ledger control	6,000	
Purchases ledger control		8,000
Value Added Tax		2,000
	255,000	255,000

*Only the closing inventory is included in the trial balance because cost of sales has already been calculated.

Notes at 31 December 20-5:

- depreciation is to be charged on the shop fittings at 10 per cent per year

- Steven Hill is to receive a partnership salary of £15,000

- allow interest on partners' capital: James £3,800 and Hill £3,200

- remaining profits and losses are to be shared equally

Task 1

Prepare the partnership financial statements for the year ended 31 December 20-5, using the extended trial balance method.

Task 2

Show the partners' capital and current accounts for the year ended 31 December 20-5.

Task 3

Prepare the partnership financial statements for the year ended 31 December 20-5 in the conventional format.

Task 4

On receiving the accounts, John James asks a question about the partners' current accounts. He wants to know why the balances brought down at the start of the year for the two partners are on opposite sides.

Draft a note to John James explaining:

- what the balance on a partner's current account represents

- what a debit balance on a partner's current account means

- what a credit balance on a partner's current account means

6.6   You have the following information about a partnership business:

- the financial year ends on 31 March

- the partners are Ian, Jim and Kay

- partners' annual salaries:
Ian	£20,500
Jim	£14,500
Kay	£10,250

- partners' capital account balances as at 31 March 20-5:
Ian	£30,000
Jim	£40,000
Kay	£20,000

- interest on partners' capital for the year:
Ian	£1,500
Jim	£2,000
Kay	£1,000

- the partners share the remaining profit of £22,000 as follows:
Ian	40%
Jim	40%
Kay	20%

- partners' drawings for the year:
Ian	£30,000
Jim	£25,000
Kay	£14,000

You are to prepare the current accounts for the partners for the year ended 31 March 20-5. Show clearly the balances carried down. You MUST enter zeros where appropriate in order to obtain full mark. Do **not** use brackets, minus signs or dashes.

Current accounts	Ian £	Jim £	Kay £		Ian £	Jim £	Kay £
Balance b/d	0	0	200	Balance b/d	0	900	0

6.7 This Activity is about preparing a partnership statement of financial position.

You are preparing the statement of financial position for the DE Partnership for the year ended 31 March 20-2. The partners are Don and Eve.

All the necessary year end adjustments have been made, except for the transfer of profit to the current accounts of the partners.

Before sharing profits the balances of the partners' current accounts are:

- Don £750 credit

- Eve £400 debit

Each partner is entitled to £4,000 profit share.

(a) Calculate the balance of each partner's current account after sharing profits. Fill in the answers below.

Current account balance: Don	£
Current account balance: Eve	£

Note: these balances will need to be transferred into the statement of financial position of the partnership which follows.

You have the following trial balance. All the necessary year end adjustments have been made.

(b) Prepare a statement of financial position for the partnership as at 31 March 20-2. You need to use the partners' current account balances that you have just calculated. Do **not** use brackets, minus signs or dashes.

DE Partnership
Trial balance as at 31 March 20-2

	Dr £	Cr £
Accruals		550
Administration expenses	28,180	
Allowance for doubtful debts		1,100
Allowance for doubtful debts: adjustment	110	
Bank	11,520	
Capital account – Don		25,000
Capital account – Eve		20,000
Cash	150	
Closing inventory	15,790	15,790
Current account – Don		750
Current account – Eve	400	
Depreciation charge	3,250	
Disposal of non-current asset	650	
Machinery at cost	35,500	
Machinery: accumulated depreciation		12,150
Opening inventory	11,650	
Purchases	70,250	
Purchases ledger control		18,720
Sales revenue		125,240
Sales ledger control	25,690	
Selling expenses	18,940	
Value Added Tax		2,780
Total	222,080	222,080

DE Partnership
Statement of financial position as at 31 March 20-2

	Cost £	Accumulated depreciation £	Carrying amount £
Non-current assets			
Current assets			
Current liabilities			
Net current assets			
Net assets			
Financed by:	**Don**	**Eve**	**Total**

7 Changes in partnerships

this chapter covers...

In this chapter we continue our study of partnerships by looking at the principles involved and the accounting entries, for:

- *admission of a new partner*

- *retirement of a partner*

- *changes in profit-sharing ratios*

Before we look at these, we need to consider the goodwill of the business, which features in the changes listed above.

GOODWILL

The statement of financial position of a partnership, like that of many businesses, rarely indicates the true value of the business as a going concern: usually the recorded figures underestimate the worth of a business. There are two main reasons for this:

■ **Faithful representation** – if there is doubt about the value of assets, they are usually stated at the lower figure, but without bias

■ **Goodwill** – a going concern business (ie one that continues to trade successfully) will often have a value of goodwill, because of various factors, eg the trade that has been built up, the reputation of the business, the location of the business, the skill of the workforce, and the success at developing new products

definition of goodwill

Goodwill can be defined formally in accounting terms as:

the difference between the value of a business as a whole, and the net value of its separate assets and liabilities.

For example, an existing business is bought for £500,000, with the separate assets and liabilities being worth £450,000 net; goodwill is, therefore, £50,000.

Thus goodwill has a value as an intangible non-current asset to the owner or owners of a going concern business, whether or not it is recorded on the statement of financial position. As you will see in the sections which follow, a valuation has to be placed on goodwill when changes take place in a partnership.

valuation of goodwill

The valuation of goodwill is always subject to negotiation between the people concerned if, for instance, a partnership business is to be sold. It is, most commonly, based on the profits of the business – eg the average profit over the last, say, three years and multiplied by an agreed figure, perhaps six times.

We will now see how goodwill is created when changes are made to partnerships, such as the admission of a new partner or retirement of an existing partner. For these changes, a value for goodwill is agreed and this amount is temporarily debited to goodwill account, and credited to the partners' capital accounts in their profit-sharing ratio. After the change in the partnership, it is usual practice for the goodwill to be written off – the partners' capital accounts are debited and goodwill account is credited. Thus a 'nil' balance remains on goodwill account and, therefore, it is not recorded on the partnership statement of financial position. This is the method commonly followed when changes are made to partnerships.

ADMISSION OF A NEW PARTNER

A new partner – who can only be admitted with the consent of all existing partners – is normally charged a premium for goodwill. This is because the new partner will start to share in the profits of the business immediately and will benefit from the goodwill established by the existing partners. If the business was to be sold shortly after the admission of a new partner, a price will again be agreed for goodwill and this will be shared amongst all the partners (including the new partner).

To make allowance for this benefit it is necessary to make double-entry adjustments in the partners' capital accounts. The most common way of doing this is to use a goodwill account which is opened by the old partners with the agreed valuation of goodwill and, immediately after the admission of the new partner, is closed by transfer to the partners' capital accounts, including that of the new partner.

The procedures on admission of a new partner are:

■ **agree a valuation for goodwill**

■ **old partners: goodwill created**
- debit goodwill account with the amount of goodwill
- credit partners' capital accounts (in their old profit-sharing ratio) with the amount of goodwill

■ **old partners + new partner: goodwill written off**
- debit partners' capital accounts (in their new profit-sharing ratio) with the amount of goodwill
- credit goodwill account with the amount of goodwill

The effect of this is to charge the new partner with a premium for goodwill.

Case Study

AL AND BEN:
ADMISSION OF A NEW PARTNER

situation

Al and Ben are in partnership sharing profits and losses equally. Their statement of financial position as at 31 December 20-1 is as follows:

AL AND BEN	
STATEMENT OF FINANCIAL POSITION as at 31 December 20-1	
	£
Net assets	80,000
Capital accounts:	
Al	45,000
Ben	35,000
	80,000

On 1 January 20-2 the partners agree to admit Col into the partnership, with a new profit-sharing ratio of Al (2), Ben (2) and Col (1). Goodwill has been agreed at a valuation of £25,000. Col will bring £20,000 of cash into the business as his capital, part of which represents a premium for goodwill.

solution

The accounting procedures on the admission of Col into the partnership are as follows:

- goodwill has been valued at £25,000

- old partners: goodwill created

  – debit goodwill account

capital – Al	£12,500
capital – Ben	£12,500

  – credit capital accounts (in their old profit-sharing ratio)

goodwill – Al	£12,500
goodwill – Ben	£12,500

- old partners + new partner: goodwill written off

  – debit capital accounts (in their new profit-sharing ratio)

goodwill – Al	£10,000
goodwill – Ben	£10,000
goodwill – Col	£5,000

  – credit goodwill account | £25,000

capital – Al	£10,000
capital – Ben	£10,000
capital – Col	£5,000

The capital accounts of the partners, after the above transactions have been recorded, appear as:

Dr				Partners' capital accounts				Cr
	Al	**Ben**	**Col**		**Al**	**Ben**	**Col**
	£	£	£		£	£	£
Goodwill	10,000	10,000	5,000	Balances b/d	45,000	35,000	-
Balances c/d	47,500	37,500	15,000	Goodwill	12,500	12,500	-
				Bank	-	-	20,000
	57,500	47,500	20,000		57,500	47,500	20,000
				Balances b/d	47,500	37,500	15,000

The statement of financial position, following the admission of Col, appears as:

AL, BEN AND COL
STATEMENT OF FINANCIAL POSITION as at 1 January 20-2

	£
Net assets (£80,000 + £20,000)	100,000
Capital accounts:	
Al (£45,000 + £12,500 – £10,000)	47,500
Ben (£35,000 + £12,500 – £10,000)	37,500
Col (£20,000 – £5,000)	15,000
	100,000

In this way, the new partner has paid the existing partners a premium of £5,000 for a one-fifth share of the profits of a business with a goodwill value of £25,000.

Although a goodwill account has been used, it has been fully utilised with adjusting entries made in the capital accounts of the partners, as follows:

Dr			Goodwill account			Cr
		£				£
Capital – Al	goodwill created	12,500	Capital – Al	goodwill written off	10,000
Capital – Ben		12,500	Capital – Ben		10,000
			Capital – Col		5,000
		25,000			25,000

RETIREMENT OF A PARTNER

When a partner retires it is necessary to calculate how much is due to the partner in respect of capital and profits. The partnership agreement normally details the procedures to be followed when a partner retires. The most common procedure requires goodwill to be valued and this operates in a similar way to the admission of a new partner, as follows:

- **agree a valuation for goodwill**
- **old partners: goodwill created**
  - debit goodwill account with the amount of goodwill
  - credit partners' capital accounts (in their old profit-sharing ratio) with the amount of goodwill
- **remaining partners: goodwill written off**
  - debit partners' capital accounts (in their new profit-sharing ratio) with the amount of goodwill
  - credit goodwill account with the amount of goodwill

The effect of this is to credit the retiring partner with the amount of the goodwill built up whilst he or she was a partner. This amount, plus the retiring partner's capital and current account balances can then be paid out of the partnership bank account. (If there is insufficient money for this, it is quite usual for a retiring partner to leave some of the capital in the business as a loan, which is repaid over a period of time.)

Case Study

JAN, KAY AND LIL: RETIREMENT OF A PARTNER

situation

Jan, Kay and Lil are in partnership sharing profit and losses in the ratio of 2:2:1 respectively. Partner Jan decides to retire on 31 December 20-4 when the partnership statement of financial position is as follows:

JAN, KAY AND LIL	
STATEMENT OF FINANCIAL POSITION as at 31 December 20-4	
	£
Net assets	100,000
Capital accounts:	
Jan	35,000
Kay	45,000
Lil	20,000
	100,000

Goodwill is agreed at a valuation of £30,000. Kay and Lil are to continue in partnership and will share profits and losses in the ratio of 2:1 respectively. Jan agrees to leave £20,000 of the amount due to her as a loan to the new partnership.

solution

The accounting procedures on the retirement of Jan from the partnership are as follows:

- goodwill has been valued at £30,000

- old partners: goodwill created

  - debit goodwill account

capital – Jan	£12,000
capital – Kay	£12,000
capital – Lil	£6,000

  - credit capital accounts (in their old profit-sharing ratio of 2:2:1)

goodwill – Jan	£12,000
goodwill – Kay	£12,000
goodwill – Lil	£6,000

- remaining partners: goodwill written off

  - debit capital accounts (in their new profit-sharing ratio of 2:1)

goodwill – Kay	£20,000
goodwill – Lil	£10,000

  - credit goodwill account

capital – Kay	£20,000
capital – Lil	£10,000

The capital accounts of the partners, after the above transactions have been recorded, appear as:

Dr				**Partners' capital accounts**				Cr
	Jan	Kay	Lil		Jan	Kay	Lil
	£	£	£		£	£	£
Goodwill	–	20,000	10,000	Balances b/d	35,000	45,000	20,000
Loan	20,000			Goodwill	12,000	12,000	6,000
Bank	27,000						
Balances c/d	–	37,000	16,000				
	47,000	57,000	26,000		47,000	57,000	26,000
				Balances b/d	–	37,000	16,000

Note: After recording goodwill, the balance of Jan's capital account is £47,000 (ie £35,000 + £12,000, being her share of the goodwill). Of this, £20,000 will be retained in the business as a loan, and £27,000 will be paid to her from the partnership bank account.

The statement of financial position, after the retirement of Jan, appears as follows:

KAY AND LIL	
STATEMENT OF FINANCIAL POSITION as at 1 January 20-5	
	£
Net assets (£100,000 – £27,000 paid to Jan)	73,000
Less Loan account of Jan	20,000
	53,000
Capital accounts:	
Kay (£45,000 + £12,000 – £20,000)	37,000
Lil (£20,000 + £6,000 – £10,000)	16,000
	53,000

The effect of this is that the remaining partners have bought out Jan's £12,000 share of the goodwill of the business, ie it has cost Kay £8,000, and Lil £4,000. If the business was to be sold later, Kay and Lil would share the goodwill obtained from the sale in their new profit-sharing ratio.

CHANGES IN PROFIT-SHARING RATIOS

It may be necessary, from time-to-time, to change the profit-sharing ratios of partners. A partner's share of profits might be increased because of an increase in capital in relation to the other partners, or because of a more active role in running the business. Equally, a share of profits may be decreased if a partner withdraws capital or spends less time in the business. Clearly, the agreement of all partners is needed to make changes, and the guidance of the partnership agreement should be followed as to how the changes should be effected.

Generally, even if the partnership is to continue with the same partners, a change in the profit-sharing ratio involves establishing a figure for goodwill, and may also require revaluation of the partnership's assets and liabilities. The objective is to establish how much goodwill has been built up while the partners shared profits in their old ratios. Each partner will be credited with a value for the goodwill based on the old profit-sharing ratio and will be debited with the goodwill based on the new profit-sharing ratio.

Case Study

DES AND EVE:
CHANGES IN PROFIT-SHARING RATIOS

situation

Des and Eve are in partnership sharing profits and losses equally. The statement of financial position at 31 December 20-6 is as follows:

DES AND EVE STATEMENT OF FINANCIAL POSITION as at 31 December 20-6	
	£
Net assets	60,000
Capital accounts:	
Des	35,000
Eve	25,000
	60,000

The partners agree that, as from 1 January 20-7, Des will take a two-thirds share of the profits and losses, with Eve taking one-third. Goodwill has been valued at £30,000. The partners agree that goodwill is to be introduced into their capital accounts and then eliminated.

solution

The accounting procedures on the change in the profit-sharing ratio are as follows:

- goodwill has been valued at £30,000

- old profit-sharing ratio: goodwill created

  - debit goodwill account
capital – Des	£15,000
capital – Eve	£15,000

  - credit capital accounts (in their old profit-sharing ratio of 1:1)
goodwill – Des	£15,000
goodwill – Eve	£15,000

- new profit-sharing ratio: goodwill written off

  - debit capital accounts (in their new profit-sharing ratio of 2:1)
goodwill – Des	£20,000
goodwill – Eve	£10,000

  - credit goodwill account
capital – Des	£20,000
capital – Eve	£10,000

The capital accounts of the partners, after the above transactions have been recorded, appear as:

Dr			Partners' capital accounts			Cr
	Des	**Eve**		**Des**	**Eve**
	£	£		£	£
Goodwill	20,000	10,000	Balances b/d	35,000	25,000
Balances c/d	30,000	30,000	Goodwill	15,000	15,000
	50,000	40,000		50,000	40,000
			Balances b/d	30,000	30,000

The statement of financial position at 1 January 20-7 appears as:

DES AND EVE
STATEMENT OF FINANCIAL POSITION as at 1 January 20-7

	£
Net assets	60,000
Capital accounts:	
Des (£35,000 + £15,000 – £20,000)	30,000
Eve (£25,000 + £15,000 – £10,000)	30,000
	60,000

The effect is that Des has 'paid' Eve £5,000 to increase his share of the profits from half to two-thirds. This may seem unfair but neither partner is worse off in the event of the business being sold, assuming that the business is sold for £90,000 (£60,000 assets + £30,000 goodwill). Before the change in the profit-sharing ratio they would have received:

Des £35,000 capital + £15,000 half-share of goodwill   =   £50,000

Eve £25,000 capital + £15,000 half-share of goodwill   =   £40,000

After the change, they will receive:

Des £30,000 capital + £20,000 two-thirds share of goodwill   =   £50,000

Eve £30,000 capital + £10,000 one-third share of goodwill   =   £40,000

As far as the sale amounts are concerned, the position remains unchanged: it is only the profit-sharing ratios that will be different as from 1 January 20-7. Also, any increase in goodwill above the £30,000 figure will be shared in the new ratio.

RECORDING PARTNERSHIP CHANGES

The accounting effects of partnership changes usually have a significant impact upon partners' capital accounts and the ratio in which they share profits and losses. Before implementing changes, the accounts assistant must check that the correct actions are being taken. This may mean referring issues to the appropriate person – such as the accounts supervisor, the manager of the partnership, or one or more of the partners.

The accounts assistant must take note of:

■ the terms of the partnership agreement

■ the policies, regulations, procedures and timescales of the partnership

If there are any discrepancies or queries they should be identified and, where possible, resolved – any outstanding issues will need to be referred to the appropriate person.

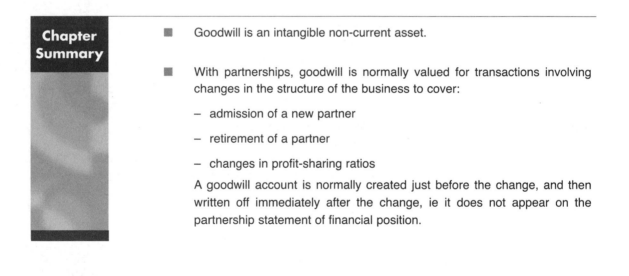

Chapter Summary

■ Goodwill is an intangible non-current asset.

■ With partnerships, goodwill is normally valued for transactions involving changes in the structure of the business to cover:

– admission of a new partner

– retirement of a partner

– changes in profit-sharing ratios

A goodwill account is normally created just before the change, and then written off immediately after the change, ie it does not appear on the partnership statement of financial position.

Key Terms

goodwill	the difference between the value of a business as a whole, and the net value of its separate assets and liabilities
goodwill account	an account to which goodwill, an intangible non-current asset, is debited
premium for goodwill	amount charged to a new partner who joins an existing partnership

Activities

7.1 Andrew and Barry are in partnership sharing profits equally. Colin is admitted to the partnership and the profit sharing ratios now become Andrew (2), Barry (2) and Colin (1). Goodwill at the time of Colin joining is valued at £50,000. What will be the goodwill adjustments to Andrew's capital account?

(a) debit £25,000, credit £25,000	
(b) debit £20,000, credit £25,000	
(c) debit £20,000, credit £20,000	
(d) debit £25,000, credit £20,000	

7.2 Jim and Maisie are in partnership sharing profits and losses in the ratio 3:2 respectively. At 31 December 20-4 the balances of their capital accounts are £60,000 and £40,000 respectively.

On 1 January 20-5, Matt is admitted into the partnership, with a new profit-sharing ratio of Jim (3), Maisie (2) and Matt (1). Goodwill has been agreed at a valuation of £48,000. Matt will bring £28,000 of cash into the business as his capital and premium for goodwill. Goodwill is to be eliminated from the accounts.

There are no other capital account transactions during 20-5.

You are to show the partners' capital accounts for the period from 31 December 20-4 to 1 January 20-6.

7.3 Reena, Sam and Tamara are in partnership sharing profits in the ratio 4:2:2 respectively. Sam is to retire on 31 August 20-8 and is to be paid the amount due to him from the bank.

The statement of financial position drawn up immediately before Sam's retirement was as follows:

	£
Non-current assets	50,000
Current assets	10,000
Bank	25,000
	85,000
Trade payables	(10,000)
	75,000
Capital accounts:	
Reena	33,000
Sam	12,000
Tamara	30,000
	75,000

Goodwill is to be valued at £16,000. No goodwill is to remain in the accounts after Sam's retirement. In the new partnership Reena and Tamara are to share profits equally.

Task 1

Prepare the partners' capital accounts, showing the amount Sam is to be paid upon retirement (dates are not required).

Task 2

Show the statement of financial position at 1 September 20-8 immediately after Sam's retirement from the partnership.

7.4 Dave and Elsa are in partnership sharing profits and losses equally. Their statement of financial position at 30 September 20-8 is as follows:

DAVE AND ELSA

STATEMENT OF FINANCIAL POSITION as at 30 September 20-8

	£
Net assets	130,000
Capital Accounts:	
Dave	80,000
Elsa	50,000
	130,000

The partners agree that, as from 1 October 20-8, Dave will take a two-thirds share of the profits and losses, with Elsa taking one-third. Goodwill has been valued at £45,000. The partners agree that goodwill is to be introduced into their capital accounts and then eliminated.

Task 1

Show the journal entries dated 1 October 20-8 to record the creation of goodwill and its subsequent elimination for the change in the profit-sharing ratio.

Task 2

Show the partners' capital accounts with the entries on 1 October 20-8 to record the change in the profit-sharing ratio.

Task 3

Show the statement of financial position of Dave and Elsa at 1 October 20-8 after the change in the profit-sharing ratio.

7.5 Jean and David are in partnership. Profit for the year ended 31 December 20-1 is £32,700 before appropriation of profit. Their partnership agreement allows for the following:

- partnership salaries
  - Jean   £14,000
  - David £8,000

- profit share
  - Jean   one-half
  - David one-half

Notes:

- interest on capital for the year:
  - Jean   £500
  - David £600
- drawings for the year: Jean £18,600, David £14,200

Task 1

Prepare the partnership appropriation account for Jean and David for the year ended 31 December 20-1.

Task 2

Update the current accounts (on the next page) for the partnership for the year ended 31 December 20-1. Show clearly the balances carried down.

Dr   Partners' current accounts   Cr

20-1		Jean	David	20-1		Jean	David
		£	£			£	£
1 Jan	Balance b/d	–	1,250	1 Jan	Balance b/d	2,400	–

7.6   You have the following information about a partnership:

The partners are Kay and Lee.

- Mel was admitted to the partnership on 1 April 20-1 when she introduced £30,000 to the bank account.

- profit share, effective until 31 March 20-1:
    - Kay   50%
    - Lee   50%

- profit share, effective from 1 April 20-1:
    - Kay   40%
    - Lee   40%
    - Mel   20%

- goodwill was valued at £24,000 on 31 March 20-1

- goodwill is to be introduced into the partners' capital accounts on 31 March and then eliminated on 1 April

(a)   Prepare the capital account for Mel, the new partner, showing clearly the balance carried down as at 1 April 20-1. (Dates are not required.)

Capital account – Mel

		Balance b/d	0

(b)   Complete the following sentence by circling the appropriate phrase in each case:

Goodwill can be defined as the difference between **(the value of the business/the balance at bank)**, and the **(accumulated depreciation/net value)** of the separate **(trade receivables and trade payables/assets and liabilities)**.

8 Introduction to company financial statements

this chapter covers...

In this book we have focused on the financial statements of sole traders and partnerships. We now turn to the statements of limited companies – in preparation for your studies at AAT Professional Diploma – and cover:

- *the main sources of regulation governing company financial statements*

- *a recap on the financial reporting standards which provide guidance for property, plant and equipment, and inventories*

- *the presentation of company financial statements, including:*

    - *Companies Act requirements*

    - *accounting principles (concepts)*

    - *accounting policies*

- *the statement of profit or loss*

- *the statement of financial position*

REGULATION OF COMPANY FINANCIAL STATEMENTS

Preparation of the financial statements of limited companies (ltd) and public limited companies (plc) is a natural progression from the statements of sole traders and partnerships.

The layout of company financial statements is similar but more complex – so accountants preparing them need to maintain an up-to-date knowledge of relevant legislation and accounting standards, in particular the regulatory requirements of:

- the Companies Act 2006

- Financial Reporting Standards (FRSs) or International Financial Reporting Standards (IFRSs)

FRSs are the UK domestic accounting standards, issued by the Financial Reporting Council and used by smaller limited companies. IFRSs and also IASs (International Accounting Standards) are the international standards, issued by the International Accounting Standards Board and widely used by larger companies.

A company's financial statements must be prepared in accordance with the Companies Act and with either UK accounting standards or international financial reporting standards.

Two international financial reporting standards – which have been seen in earlier studies for AAT Advanced Diploma 'Advanced Bookkeeping' provide examples of regulation governing company financial statements adopting IFRS. They are:

> **IAS 2, Inventories** – sets out the accounting techniques for valuing inventories, generally at the lower of cost and net realisable value

> **IAS 16, Property, plant and equipment** – sets out the accounting treatment for non-current assets, and how to show the carrying amount in the statement of financial position, after deducting accumulated depreciation

The preparation of company financial statements is a more regulated process than that for sole traders and partnerships. The basic structures are the same but many additional considerations must be applied.

PRESENTATION OF COMPANY FINANCIAL STATEMENTS

Limited companies that adopt international financial reporting standards – that is larger companies and an increasing number of smaller companies – must set out their financial statements in a certain way. This is to ensure comparability with previous accounting periods and with other companies.

The information required to be shown on the statement of profit or loss and statement of financial position is given in International Accounting Standard No. 1 (IAS 1), which is entitled 'Presentation of financial statements'. Each financial statement and the information to be shown will be considered in more detail in the following sections.

IAS 1 also requires companies to include a statement of cash flows as part of their financial statements. This statement links profit from the statement of profit or loss with changes in assets and liabilities in the statement of financial position, and shows the effect on the cash of the company. Statements of cash flows are studied in detail at AAT Professional Diploma, 'Financial Statements of Limited Companies'.

Companies Act requirements

The Companies Act 2006 requires company directors to keep adequate accounting records sufficient to show and explain the company's transactions and to disclose the financial position. The directors of a company must prepare financial statements at least annually (although under some circumstances the statements may cover periods of up to eighteen months) which must be approved by the company's board of directors and signed, on behalf of the board, by a director whose signature must be on the statement of financial position.

The Companies Act also sets out requirements for certain information to be disclosed as part of the financial statements, eg employee numbers and costs, directors' benefits and remuneration, etc. The directors also prepare a directors' report which includes a review of the activities of the company over the past year and of likely developments in the future. The directors must report annually to the company's shareholders on the way that they have run the company on behalf of the shareholders.

The annual financial statements and directors' report are filed with the Registrar of Companies where they are available for public inspection.

accounting principles (concepts)

IAS 1 requires that companies comply with accounting principles (concepts) as follows:

- going concern – financial statements are prepared on the basis that the company will continue to operate in the foreseeable future
- accruals – financial statements are prepared on the basis that income and expenses incurred in the same accounting period are matched
- materiality – each material class of similar items is to be shown separately in the financial statements

accounting policies

IAS 1 requires that financial statements should meet the requirements of fair presentation and compliance with international financial reporting standards. As a part of fair presentation, IAS 1 requires companies:

- to select and apply accounting policies
- to present information, including accounting policies, so as to provide relevant, reliable, comparable and understandable information (the qualitative characteristics of useful financial information – see Chapter 2)
- where necessary, to provide additional information to enable users to understand particular transactions

Accounting policies cover the specific accounting methods selected by the directors and applied by a company in the preparation of its financial statements, for example:

- inventories valuation
- depreciation of property, plant and equipment

STATEMENT OF PROFIT OR LOSS

A statement of profit or loss that meets the requirements of IAS 1 does not have to detail every single overhead or expense incurred – to do so would be to disclose important management information to competitors. Instead, the main items are summarised, and a typical statement for a trading company will include the following:

- revenue from sales
- cost of sales
- distribution costs
- administrative expenses

- finance costs
- tax expense*

*Note that taxation is charged in the statement of profit or loss of a company because it is a liability of the company as a separate legal entity in contrast to sole traders and partnerships, where tax is a liability of the sole owner or each partner.

Further detail is provided to give information relevant to an understanding of financial performance.

The statement of profit or loss concludes by showing the profit or loss for the period attributable to equity holders (ie due to the shareholders).

Expenses must be analysed either by nature (raw materials, employee costs, depreciation, etc) or by function (cost of sales, distribution costs, and administrative expenses) – depending on which provides the more reliable and relevant information. The analysis by nature is often appropriate for manufacturing companies, while the analysis by function is commonly used by trading companies. The example statement of profit or loss on the next page shows analysis by function.

Much of the detail shown in the statement of profit or loss is summarised. For example:

- revenue incorporates the figures for sales and sales returns
- cost of sales includes opening inventories, purchases, purchases returns, carriage inwards and closing inventories
- distribution costs include warehouse costs, post and packing, delivery drivers' wages, running costs of delivery vehicles, depreciation of delivery vehicles, etc
- administrative expenses include office costs, rent and rates, heating and lighting, depreciation of office equipment, etc

An example of a statement of profit or loss (with specimen figures) which complies with IAS 1 is shown on the next page, with expenses analysed by function.

Note that the statement of changes in equity, of which an extract is shown here, demonstrates how profit for the year is added to the brought forward balance of retained earnings (profits from earlier years that have been retained in the company), while dividends paid to shareholders during the year are deducted. The resultant balance of retained earnings at the year end is shown in the statement of financial position as a reserve of the company.

XYZ PLC
Statement of profit or loss
for the year ended 31 December 20-9

	£000
Revenue	30,000
Cost of sales	16,000
Gross profit	14,000
Distribution costs	5,000
Administrative expenses	4,000
Profit/(loss) from operations	5,000
Finance costs	1,000
Profit/(loss) before tax	4,000
Tax expense	1,500
Profit/(loss) for the year attributable to equity holders	2,500

STATEMENT OF CHANGES IN EQUITY (EXTRACT)

Retained earnings	
Balance at 1 January 20-9	2,400
Profit for the year attributable to equity holders	2,500
	4,900
Dividends paid	600
Balance at 31 December 20-9	4,300

STATEMENT OF FINANCIAL POSITION

IAS 1 specifies the items to be shown on the face of the statement of financial position as a minimum. The Standard does not, however, state the order in which the items are to be presented.

The items to be shown on the face of the balance sheet include:

- property, plant and equipment (shown at carrying amount)
- intangible assets, eg goodwill (shown at carrying amount)
- inventories
- trade and other receivables
- cash and cash equivalents, ie bank and cash balances
- trade and other payables
- tax liabilities
- issued capital and reserves

Further detail is given about items shown in the statement of financial position – either on the face of the statement or in the notes. Examples include:

- property, plant and equipment may be shown by different classes – such as property, machinery, motor vehicles, office equipment, etc
- trade and other receivables may be split into amounts due from trade customers, prepayments of expenses, etc
- inventories can be sub-classified into raw materials, work-in-progress, finished goods, etc
- trade and other payables may be split into amounts owing to trade suppliers, accruals of expenses, etc
- issued share capital and reserves can be shown by classes of shares and reserves

An example of a statement of financial position which complies with IAS 1 is shown on the next page.

IAS 1 does not set out a required format for statements of financial position: assets can be presented first, balanced against liabilities, issued capital and reserves; or, in a version common in the UK, non-current assets can be followed by net current assets (current assets minus current liabilities), then non-current liabilities, all balanced against issued capital and reserves. This latter layout is shown in the example statement of financial position (with specimen figures).

XYZ PLC
Statement of Financial Position
as at 31 December 20-9

	£000	£000
Non-current assets		
Intangible: Goodwill (at carrying amount)		50
Property, plant and equipment (at carrying amount)		9,750
		9,800
Current assets		
Inventories		1,190
Trade and other receivables		1,600
Cash and cash equivalents		10
Total current assets		2,800
Current Liabilities		
Trade and other payables	950	
Tax liabilities	850	
Total current liabilities		1,800
Net current assets		1,000
		10,800
Non-current liabilities		
Bank loans		1,600
Net assets		9,200
Issued capital and reserves		
Issued capital		4,000
Share premium*		400
Revaluation reserve**		500
Retained earnings		4,300
Total issued capital and reserves		9,200

*shares will have been issued by the company in the past at higher than their nominal value and the balance credited to share premium account

**property will have been revalued upwards and the increase credited to revaluation reserve account

■ Accountants preparing company financial statements need to maintain an up-to-date knowledge of relevant legislation and accounting standards.

■ The main sources of regulation governing company financial statements are:
- the Companies Act 2006
- Financial Reporting Standards (FRSs) or International Financial Reporting Standards (IFRSs).

■ IAS 2, Inventories, sets out the accounting techniques to be used when valuing inventories.

■ IAS 16, Property, plant and equipment, sets out the accounting treatment for non-current assets.

■ IAS 1, Presentation of financial statements, sets out the information required to be shown on a company's statement of profit or loss and statement of financial position.

■ The Companies Act 2006 sets out the responsibilities of directors for keeping accounting records and preparing and presenting financial statements.

■ IAS requires that companies comply with the accounting principles (concepts) of:
- going concern
- accruals
- materiality

■ The directors of a company select and apply accounting policies so as to provide relevant, reliable, comparable and understandable information.

■ The statement of profit or loss for a trading company typically includes the following:
- revenue
- cost of sales
- distribution costs
- administrative expenses
- finance costs
- tax expenses

■ A statement of changes in equity follows the statement of profit or loss, an extract of which will show profit for the year, dividends paid, and the balance of retained earnings at the year end, which goes through to the statement of financial position.

■ IAS 1 specifies the items to be shown on the face of the statement of financial position.

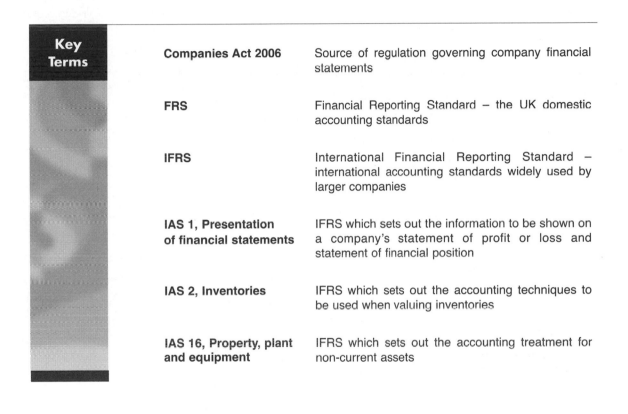

Key Terms		
Companies Act 2006	Source of regulation governing company financial statements
FRS	Financial Reporting Standard – the UK domestic accounting standards
IFRS	International Financial Reporting Standard – international accounting standards widely used by larger companies
IAS 1, Presentation of financial statements	IFRS which sets out the information to be shown on a company's statement of profit or loss and statement of financial position
IAS 2, Inventories	IFRS which sets out the accounting techniques to be used when valuing inventories
IAS 16, Property, plant and equipment	IFRS which sets out the accounting treatment for non-current assets

Activities

8.1 What are the main responsibilities of the directors of a limited company in respect of the regulations governing company financial statements?

8.2 The directors of Beacon Ltd, a recently-formed trading company, seek your guidance. How would you advise them on the following:

(a) What items should we show on the face of the statement of profit or loss?

(b) How should we analyse our expenses for the statement of profit or loss?

8.3 Explain where the following items appear in a limited company's financial statements:

– tax expense
– property, plant and equipment
– finance costs
– tax liabilities
– retained earnings

8.4 Which **one** of the items below prescribes the format of financial statements for an organisation adopting IFRS?

(a)	IAS 1	
(b)	IAS 2	
(c)	IAS 16	

8.5 Which of the following statements are **true** for a limited company?

1. Expenses must be analysed either by nature or by function.
2. IAS 1 sets out a required format for statements of financial position.
3. A directors' report includes likely developments for the future.

(a)	1 and 2	
(b)	2 and 3	
(c)	1 and 3	
(d)	All of them	

Answers to chapter activities

CHAPTER 1: BUSINESS ORGANISATIONS

1.1   Advantages of a sole trader business:
- the owner has independence
- all profits belong to the owner
- personal service and supervision are available at all times
- the business is easy to establish legally

Disadvantages of a sole trader business:
- the owner has unlimited liability
- all losses are the owner's responsibility
- expansion is limited
- there may be limited finance – ploughing back profits, or borrowing from a lender
- the owner usually has to work long hours, with few holidays
- if the owner becomes ill the business will be affected

Possible future developments:
- form a partnership
- form a limited company

1.2   **(a)**   A partnership is a group of individuals working together in business with a view to making a profit.

   (b)   A limited liability partnership differs from an ordinary partnership:
- legislation is the Limited Liability Partnership Act, 2000
- it is incorporated and has a separate legal entity from the members
- members are able to limit their liability for the debts of the business
- it has two or more 'designated members' who are responsible for ensuring that the legal and accounting requirements are carried out
- an Annual Return has to be submitted to Companies House, where it is in the public domain

1.3   **(a)**   The shareholders own the company.

   (b)   The directors run the company on behalf of the shareholders.

   (c)   If the company becomes insolvent the liability of shareholders for debts is limited to the amount of their investment.

1.4   **(a)**   Incorporation means a company or other organisation being formed into a legal entity separate from its owners. Examples are limited liability partnerships (LLPs) and limited companies.

   (b)   Advantages of incorporation (two from):
- a limit on the liability of members (LLPs) and shareholders (limited companies) for the debts of the business
- the continuing existence of the business as a separate legal entity
- an enhancement of the credibility of the business
- access to finance may be easier than a sole trader
- transfer of ownership may be easier than a sole trader

Disadvantages of incorporation (two from):
- more complex requirements to set up the business
- higher costs of keeping up with record keeping and annual returns
- information filed with Companies House is in the public domain
- business finances must be kept entirely separate from those of the owners

1.5 **(a)** A charity is an organisation which uses its resources to fund charitable activities under its control.

(b) The main rules governing charities are:
- they must follow charity law, the Charities Act 2011, and the Charity Commission regulations
- for financial reporting they must follow either the Statement of Recommended Practice, or Financial Reporting Standard 102
- their purpose must be for the public benefit
- they are governed by a trust deed
- they are run by trustees
- they are independent of other organisations

1.6 Points to identify include:

(a) sole traders – the owner
partnerships – the partners
limited liability partnerships – the members
limited companies – the shareholders
charities – run by trustees for the public benefit

(b) sole traders – the owner
partnerships – all partners entitled to take an active role
limited liability partnerships – all members entitled to take an active role
limited companies – run by directors on behalf of shareholders
charities – run by trustees

(c) sole traders – owner is liable for entire debt of business
partnerships – partners are each liable for entire debt of partnership
limited liability partnerships – members can lose up to their investment in the LLP
limited companies – shareholders can lose up to their investment in the company
charities – for unincorporated charities, trustees may be liable for debts of the charity

(d) sole traders – income tax on profits paid by the owner
partnerships – each partner liable for income tax on their share of profits
limited liability partnerships – each member liable for income tax on their share of profits
limited companies – corporation tax paid on the profits of the company
charities – exempt from tax when income is used for charitable purposes

CHAPTER 2: FRAMEWORK OF ACCOUNTING

2.1

User	Use of Information
Owner	• To see how much profit has been made • To see how much can be paid out in drawings/dividends • To see the net asset value of the business • To assess if the business will continue in the foreseeable future
Lender	• To see how much profit has been made • To check that the business will be able to make interest payments and repayments • To assess how much of the business is being funded by the lender • To see what security is available to cover loans
Employee	• To assess whether the business is able to pay wages and salaries • To consider whether the business will continue to offer employment in the future

2.2 **(a)** • business entity
  • materiality
  • going concern
  • accruals

(b) • internal control – to ensure that the financial records are accurate and that the financial statements show the true position of the business
  • measuring business performance – so that financial reports and statements can be compared
  • obtaining credit/financing – providing lenders with the current financial position of the business
  • statutory requirements – providing information for tax and other purposes when required to do so by law

2.3

Statement	Accounting Principle
Some items are of such low value that it is not worthwhile recording them separately.	Materiality
The financial statements record and report on the activities of one particular business.	Business entity
Income and expenses are matched so that they relate to the same goods or services and the same accounting period.	Accruals
The presumption is that the business to which the financial statements relate will continue to trade in the foreseeable future.	Going concern

2.4   **(a)**   1   Relevance

2   Faithful representation

(b)   For information to be relevant it must:

- be useful to users of financial statements
- be material

For the faithful representation of information it must:

- correspond to the effect of transactions or events
- as far as possible be complete, neutral and free from error

2.5   (a), (d), (e) and (g) are correct

2.6   **(a)**   'Material misstatement' is when information contained in the financial statements is untrue – whether accidentally or intentionally – and could influence the economic decisions of users.

(b)

Material misstatement	Economic consequence to users
Profit is overstated	• Investors may decide to invest in the business • The owner takes increased drawings/dividends • More tax to pay to HM Revenue & Customs
Assets are overvalued	• A lender makes loans to the business using the asset values as security • Investors decide to invest in the business
Sales turnover is overstated	• More VAT than necessary is paid to HM Revenue & Customs • May lead to profit being overstated

2.7   **(a)**   The five ethical principles to be followed when preparing financial statements are:

- integrity
- objectivity
- professional competence and due care
- confidentiality
- professional behaviour

(b)

Situation	Relevant ethical principle
The owner of the business argues that expenses should be increased so as to show a lower profit figure.	Objectivity
The financial statements show a misleading figure for depreciation so as to show a lower profit figure.	Integrity
The accounts trainee, who has only recently started in work, is given the financial statements to complete.	Professional competence and due care
Your friend, who works for the business whose financial statements you have just prepared, wants to know how much profit was made.	Confidentiality
The accountant preparing the financial statements works in an honest and truthful way.	Professional behaviour

CHAPTER 3: PREPARING FINANCIAL STATEMENTS

3.1 **(a)**   £23,480

(b)

	Debit	Credit	No change
Non-current assets	✓		
Trade receivables			✓
Trade payables		✓	
Bank			✓
Capital			✓

(c)   (b)   A bank overdraft

3.2

NICK JOHNSON

STATEMENT OF PROFIT OR LOSS

for the year ended 31 December 20-3

	£	£
Sales revenue		310,000
Opening inventory	25,000	
Purchases	210,000	
	235,000	
Less Closing inventory	21,000	
Cost of sales		214,000
Gross profit		96,000
Less expenses:		
Administration expenses	12,400	
Wages	41,000	
Rent paid	7,500	
Telephone	1,000	
Interest paid	9,000	
Travel expenses	1,100	
		72,000
Profit for the year		24,000

STATEMENT OF FINANCIAL POSITION as at 31 December 20-3

	£	£	£
Non-current assets			
Premises			200,000
Machinery			40,000
			240,000
Current assets			
Inventory (closing)		21,000	
Trade receivables		31,000	
Bank		900	
Cash		100	
Total current assets		53,000	
Current liabilities			
Trade payables	29,000		
Value Added Tax	4,000		
Total current liabilities		33,000	
Net current assets			20,000
			260,000
Non-current liabilities			
Loan from bank			100,000
Net assets			160,000
Financed by:			
Capital			
Opening capital			150,000
Add Profit for the year			24,000
			174,000
Less Drawings			14,000
Closing capital			160,000

3.3

ALAN HARRIS
STATEMENT OF PROFIT OR LOSS
for the year ended 30 JUNE 20-4

	£	£
Sales revenue		85,500
Opening inventory	13,250	
Purchases	55,000	
	68,250	
Less Closing inventory	18,100	
Cost of sales		50,150
Gross profit		35,350
Less expenses:		
Administration expenses	850	
Wages	9,220	
Rent paid	1,200	
Telephone	680	
Interest paid	120	
Travel expenses	330	
		12,400
Profit for the year		22,950

STATEMENT OF FINANCIAL POSITION
as at 30 June 20-4

	£	£	£
Non-current assets			
Premises			65,000
Vehicle			5,250
			70,250
Current assets			
Inventory (closing)		18,100	
Trade receivables		1,350	
Bank		2,100	
Cash		600	
Total current assets		22,150	
Current liabilities			
Trade payables	6,400		
Value Added Tax	1,150		
Total current liabilities		7,550	
Net current assets			14,600
Net assets			84,850
Financed by:			
Capital			
Opening capital			70,000
Add Profit for the year			22,950
			92,950
Less Drawings			8,100
Closing capital			84,850

3.4

CHRISTINE LORRAINE
STATEMENT OF PROFIT OR LOSS
for the year ended 30 June 20-1

	£	£	£
Sales revenue			175,000
Less Sales returns			4,100
Net sales revenue			170,900
Opening inventory		15,140	
Purchases	102,000		
Add Carriage in	1,210		
	103,210		
Less Purchases returns	8,300		
Net purchases		94,910	
		110,050	
Less Closing inventory		18,350	
Cost of sales			91,700
Gross profit			79,200
Add income: Discounts received			790
			79,990
Less expenses:			
Discounts allowed		1,460	
Carriage out		5,680	
Other expenses		58,230	
			65,370
Profit for the year			14,620

CHAPTER 4: INCOMPLETE RECORDS ACCOUNTING

4.1   (c)   £260,000

4.2   (b)   £77,000 **Note:** sales are £100,000 net of VAT

4.3   (d)   £21,100

4.4   £

    (a)   •   receipts from sales   153,500
                •   add trade receivables at year end   2,500
                •   **sales for year**   156,000

    (b)   •   payments to suppliers   95,000
                •   add trade payables at year end   65,000
                •   **purchases for year**   160,000

    (c)   •   payments for rent and rates   8,750
                •   less rent prepaid at 31 Dec 20-4   250
                •   **rent and rates for year**   8,500

                •   payments for wages   15,000
                •   add wages accrued at 31 Dec 20-4   550
                •   **wages for year**   15,550

    (d)   JANE PRICE
                           STATEMENT OF PROFIT OR LOSS
                           for the year ended 31 December 20-4

                                                                       £   £

    Sales revenue   156,000
    Purchases   160,000
    Less Closing inventory   73,900

    Cost of sales   86,100
    Gross profit   69,900

    Less expenses:
        Advertising   4,830
        Rent and rates   8,500
        Wages   15,550
        Administration expenses   5,000
        Depreciation charge: shop fittings   10,000

                                                                                              43,880
    Profit for the year   26,020

(e)

JANE PRICE
STATEMENT OF FINANCIAL POSITION
as at 31 December 20-4

Non-current assets	Cost	Accumulated depreciation	Carrying amount
	£	£	£
Shop fittings	50,000	10,000	40,000
Current assets			
Inventory		73,900	
Trade receivables		2,500	
Prepayment of rent		250	
Bank*		19,900	
Total current assets		96,550	
Current liabilities			
Trade payables	65,000		
Accrual of wages	550		
Total current liabilities		65,550	
Net current assets			31,000
Net assets			71,000
Financed by:			
Capital			
Opening capital (introduced at start of year)			60,000
Add Profit for the year			26,020
			86,020
Less Drawings			15,020
Closing capital			71,000

*Cash book summary:

		£
•	total receipts for year	213,500
•	less total payments for year	193,600
•	**balance at year end**	19,900

4.5

JAMES HARVEY
CALCULATION OF GOODS FOR OWN USE FOR THE YEAR

Cost of sales is:

$$£180,000 \quad \times \quad \frac{100 - 30}{100} \quad = \quad £126,000$$

Opening inventory	£21,500
+ Purchases	£132,000
− Closing inventory	£25,000
	£128,500

With cost of sales calculated at £126,000 (above) the closing inventory is estimated to be £27,500. The actual closing inventory is £25,000 so the goods taken by the owner for own use are:

£27,500 estimated inventory − £25,000 actual inventory **= £2,500 drawings.**

4.6 **(a)**

•	receipts from sales	121,000
•	less trade receivables at beginning of year	36,000
•	add irrecoverable debts written off during year	550
•	add trade receivables at end of year	35,000
•	**sales for year**	120,550

(b)

•	payments to suppliers	62,500
•	less trade payables at beginning of year	32,500
•	add trade payables at end of year	30,000
•	**purchases for year**	60,000

(c)

•	payments for administration expenses	30,000
•	less accrual at beginning of year	500
•	add accrual at end of year	700
•	**administration expenses for year**	30,200

(d)

COLIN SMITH
STATEMENT OF PROFIT OR LOSS
for the year ended 30 June 20-5

	£	£
Sales revenue		120,550
Opening inventory	25,000	
Purchases	60,000	
	85,000	
Less Closing inventory	27,500	
Cost of sales		57,500
Gross profit		63,050
Less expenses:		
Administration expenses	30,200	
Depreciation charge: fixtures and fittings	5,000	
Irrecoverable debts	550	
		35,750
Profit for the year		27,300

(e)

COLIN SMITH
STATEMENT OF FINANCIAL POSITION as at 30 June 20-5

Non-current assets	Cost	Accumulated depreciation	Carrying amount
	£	£	£
Fixtures and fittings	50,000	15,000	35,000
Current assets			
Inventory		27,500	
Trade receivables		35,000	
Bank		1,210	
Total current assets		63,710	
Current liabilities			
Trade payables	30,000		
Accrual of administration expenses	700		
Total current liabilities		30,700	
Net current assets			33,010
Net assets			68,010
Financed by:			
Capital			
Opening capital*			69,500
Add Profit for the year			27,300
			96,800
Less Drawings			28,790
Closing capital			68,010

		£
*Opening capital:		
• assets at 1 July 20-4		102,500
• less liabilities at 1 July 20-4		33,000
• **capital at 1 July 20-4**		69,500

4.7 **(a)** **Sales ledger control account**

Balance b/d	20,400	Bank	192,650
Sales day book	201,600	Discounts allowed	2,250
		Balance c/d	27,100
	222,000		222,000

(b) **VAT control account**

Purchases day book	19,200	Balance b/d	3,050
Selling expenses	2,480	Sales day book	33,600
Bank	10,425		
Balance c/d	4,545		
	36,650		36,650

4.8

CLOTHING SUPPLIES

CALCULATION OF INVENTORY LOSS FOR THE YEAR

Cost of sales is:

$$£600,000 \ \times \ \frac{100-30}{100} \ = \ £420,000$$

Opening inventory	£20,000
+ Purchases	£430,000
− Closing inventory	£26,000
	£424,000

With cost of sales calculated at £420,000 (above) the closing inventory is estimated to be £30,000. The actual closing inventory is £26,000 so the inventory loss is:

£30,000 estimated inventory − £26,000 actual inventory **= £4,000 loss**

CHAPTER 5: SOLE TRADER FINANCIAL STATEMENTS

5.1   (c)   £10,650

5.2   (a)   £23,000

5.3   (c)   £15,950

5.4   **(a)**

Zelah Trading		
Statement of profit or loss for the year ended 31 March 20-4		
	£	£
Sales revenue		155,210
Opening inventory	4,850	
Purchases	85,260	
Closing inventory	(6,500)	
Cost of sales		83,610
Gross profit		71,600
Less expenses:		
Depreciation charge	3,400	
Discounts allowed	750	
General expenses	21,240	
Rent	8,900	
Selling expenses	27,890	
Total expenses		62,180
Profit for the year		9,420

(b)   (b)   As a current asset

(c)   (d)   The business owes HM Revenue & Customs

5.5

HELENA OSTROWSKA
STATEMENT OF PROFIT OR LOSS
for the year ended 31 March 20-5

	£	£
Sales revenue		243,820
Opening inventory	30,030	
Purchases	140,950	
	170,980	
Less Closing inventory	34,080	
Cost of sales		136,900
Gross profit		106,920
Less expenses:		
Shop wages	40,270	
Heat and light	3,470	
Rent and rates	12,045	
Depreciation charge: shop fittings	5,000	
Loss on disposal of non-current asset	850	
Irrecoverable debts	200	
		61,835
Profit for the year		45,085

STATEMENT OF FINANCIAL POSITION
as at 31 March 20-5

Non-current assets	Cost	Accumulated depreciation	Carrying amount
	£	£	£
Shop fittings	30,000	15,000	15,000
Current assets			
Inventory		34,080	
Trade receivables		46,280	
Prepayment of expenses		220	
Cash and cash equivalents (Bank)		10,180	
Total current assets		90,760	
Current liabilities			
Trade payables	24,930		
Value Added Tax	3,860		
Accrual of expenses	940		
Total current liabilities		29,730	
Net current assets			61,030
Net assets			76,030
Financed by:			
Capital			
Opening capital			62,000
Add Profit for the year			45,085
			107,085
Less Drawings			31,055
Closing capital			76,030

5.6

MARK PELISI
STATEMENT OF PROFIT OR LOSS
for the year ended 31 March 20-7

	£	£
Sales revenue		100,330
Less Sales returns		120
		100,210
Less Cost of sales		35,710
Gross profit		64,500
Add other income:		
Discounts received		240
Gain on disposal of non-current asset		160
Allowance for doubtful debts: adjustment		180
		65,080
Less expenses:		
Discounts allowed	170	
Depreciation charges: vehicles	6,000	
equipment	3,500	
Wages	24,110	
Advertising	770	
Administration expenses	14,830	
Irrecoverable debts	350	
		49,730
Profit for the year		15,350

STATEMENT OF FINANCIAL POSITION
as at 31 March 20-7

Non-current assets	Cost	Accumulated depreciation	Carrying amount
	£	£	£
Vehicles	24,000	12,500	11,500
Equipment	18,500	8,000	10,500
	42,500	20,500	22,000

Current assets			
Inventory		5,640	
Trade receivables	3,480		
Less allowance for doubtful debts	620		
		2,860	
Cash and cash equivalents (Bank)		3,800	
Total current assets		12,300	
Current liabilities			
Trade payables	2,760		
Value Added Tax	1,840		
Accrual of expenses	400		
Total current liabilities		5,000	
Net current assets			7,300
			29,300
Non-current liabilities			
Bank loan			9,000
Net assets			20,300

Financed by:			
Capital			
Opening capital			35,040
Add Profit for the year			15,350
			50,390
Less Drawings			30,090
Closing capital			20,300

CHAPTER 6: PARTNERSHIP FINANCIAL STATEMENTS

6.1 (b) Profits and losses are to be shared in proportion to capital

6.2 (a) £580 Cr

6.3 (c) Jan £500 credit; Lyn £1,550 debit

6.4

Dr			Partners' capital accounts			Cr
	Lysa	**Mark**		**Lysa**	**Mark**
20-8		£	£	20-8	£	£
31 Dec Balances c/d		50,000	40,000	1 Jan Balances b/d	50,000	40,000
20-9				20-9	
			1 Jan Balances b/d	50,000	40,000

Dr			Partners' current accounts			Cr
	Lysa	**Mark**		**Lysa**	**Mark**
20-8		£	£	20-8	£	£
31 Dec Drawings		13,000	12,250	1 Jan Balances b/d	420	1,780
31 Dec Interest on drawings		300	250	31 Dec Interest on capital	2,500	2,000
31 Dec Balance c/d		–	580	31 Dec Profit share	9,300	9,300
			31 Dec Balance c/d	1,080	–
	13,300	13,080		13,300	13,080
20-9				20-9	
1 Jan Balance b/d		1,080	–	1 Jan Balance b/d	–	580

6.5

6.5 Task 1 EXTENDED TRIAL BALANCE — J JAMES & S HILL T/A "GRAPES" — 31 DECEMBER 20-5

Account name	Ledger balances Dr £	Ledger balances Cr £	Adjustments Dr £	Adjustments Cr £	Statement of profit or loss Dr £	Statement of profit or loss Cr £	Statement of financial position Dr £	Statement of financial position Cr £
Capital account: James		38,000						38,000
Capital account: Hill		32,000						32,000
Current account: James	3,000						3,000	
Current account: Hill		1,000						1,000
Drawings: James	10,000						10,000	
Drawings: Hill	22,000						22,000	
Gross profit		89,000				89,000		
Rent and rates	7,500				7,500			
Advertising	12,000				12,000			
Heat and light	3,500				3,500			
Wages and salaries	18,000				18,000			
Sundry expenses	4,000				4,000			
Shop fittings at cost	20,000						20,000	
Shop fittings: accumulated depreciation				2,000				2,000
Bank	29,000						29,000	
Sales ledger control	6,000						6,000	
Purchases ledger control		8,000						8,000
Value Added Tax		2,000						2,000
Closing inventory: statement of financial position	35,000						35,000	
Depreciation charge			2,000		2,000			
Partnership salary: Hill					15,000			15,000
Interest on capital: James					3,800			3,800
Interest on capital: Hill					3,200			3,200
Profit/loss: James					10,000			10,000
Profit/loss: Hill					10,000			10,000
	170,000	170,000	2,000	2,000	89,000	89,000	125,000	125,000

Task 2

Dr			Partners' capital accounts			Cr
	James	**Hill**			**James**	**Hill**
20-5	£	£	20-5		£	£
31 Dec Balances c/d	38,000	32,000	1 Jan Balances b/d		38,000	32,000
20-6			20-6			
			1 Jan Balances b/d		38,000	32,000

Dr			Partners' current accounts			Cr
	James	**Hill**			**James**	**Hill**
20-5	£	£	20-5		£	£
1 Jan Balance b/d	3,000	–	1 Jan Balance b/d		–	1,000
31 Dec Drawings	10,000	22,000	31 Dec Salary		–	15,000
31 Dec Balances c/d	800	7,200	31 Dec Interest on capital		3,800	3,200
			31 Dec Profit share		10,000	10,000
	13,800	29,200			13,800	29,200
20-6			20-6			
			1 Jan Balances b/d		800	7,200

Task 3

JOHN JAMES AND STEVEN HILL IN PARTNERSHIP, TRADING AS "GRAPES"
STATEMENT OF PROFIT OR LOSS
for the year ended 31 December 20-5

	£	£
Sales revenue		174,000
Less cost of sales		85,000
Gross profit		89,000
Less expenses:		
Rent and rates	7,500	
Advertising	12,000	
Heat and light	3,500	
Wages and salaries	18,000	
Sundry expenses	4,000	
Depreciation charge: shop fittings	2,000	
		47,000
Profit for the year		42,000
Less appropriation of profit:		
Salary: Hill		15,000
Interest allowed on partners' capitals		
James £38,000 x 10%	3,800	
Hill £32,000 x 10%	3,200	
		7,000
Profit available for distribution		20,000
Profit share:		
James		10,000
Hill		10,000
Total profit distributed		20,000

STATEMENT OF FINANCIAL POSITION as at 31 December 20-5

Non-current assets	Cost	Accumulated depreciation	Carrying amount
	£	£	£
Shop fittings	20,000	2,000	18,000
Current assets			
Inventory (closing)		35,000	
Trade receivables		6,000	
Cash and cash equivalents (Bank)		29,000	
Total current assets		70,000	
Current liabilities			
Trade payables	8,000		
Value Added Tax	2,000		
Total current liabilities		10,000	
Net current assets			60,000
Net assets			78,000

Financed by:	James	Hill	Total
	£	£	£
Capital accounts	38,000	32,000	70,000
Current accounts	800	7,200	8,000
	38,800	39,200	78,000

Tutorial note: only the balances of the partners' capital and current accounts have been shown in the statement of financial position.

Task 4

- The balance on the partners' current accounts represents the balance owed or owing between the business and the individual partners after transactions such as salaries, interest on capitals, profit share, and drawings have been taken into account.

- A debit balance on a partner's current account means that the partner has drawn out more than his/her entitlement of salary, interest on capital and profit share.

- A credit balance on a partner's current account means that the partner has drawn out less than his/her entitlement of salary, interest on capital and profit share.

6.6

Current accounts	Ian £	Jim £	Kay £		Ian £	Jim £	Kay £
Balance b/d	0	0	200	Balance b/d	0	900	0
Drawings	30,000	25,000	14,000	Salaries	20,500	14,500	10,250
Balance c/d	800	1,200	1,450	Interest on capital	1,500	2,000	1,000
				Profit share	8,800	8,800	4,400
	30,800	26,200	15,650		30,800	26,200	15,650

6.7   **(a)**

Current account balance: Don	£4,750
Current account balance: Eve	£3,600

(b)   **DE Partnership**
Statement of financial position as at 31 March 20-2

Non-current assets	Cost £	Accumulated depreciation £	Carrying amount £
Machinery	35,500	12,150	23,350
Current assets			
Inventory		15,790	
Trade receivables		*24,590	
Cash and cash equivalents		**11,670	
Total current assets		52,050	
Current liabilities			
Trade payables	18,720		
Value Added Tax	2,780		
Accruals	550		
Total current liabilities		22,050	
Net current assets			30,000
Net assets			53,350

Financed by:	Don	Eve	Total
Capital accounts	25,000	20,000	45,000
Current accounts	4,750	3,600	8,350
	29,750	23,600	53,350

*sales ledger control £25,690 *minus* allowance for doubtful debts £1,100
= trade receivables £24,590
**bank £11,520 + cash £150 = cash and cash equivalents £11,670

CHAPTER 7: CHANGES IN PARTNERSHIPS

7.1 (b) debit £20,000, credit £25,000

7.2

Dr **Partners' capital accounts** Cr

		Jim	Maisie	Matt			Jim	Maisie	Matt
20-4		£	£	£	20-4		£	£	£
					31 Dec	Balances b/d	60,000	40,000	–
20-5					20-5				
1 Jan	Goodwill	24,000	16,000	8,000	1 Jan	Goodwill	28,800	19,200	–
31 Dec	Balances c/d	64,800	43,200	20,000	1 Jan	Bank			28,000
		88,800	59,200	28,000			88,800	59,200	28,000
20-6					20-6				
					1 Jan	Balances b/d	64,800	43,200	20,000

7.3 **Task 1**

Dr **Partners' capital accounts** Cr

	Reena	Sam	Tamara		Reena	Sam	Tamara
	£	£	£		£	£	£
Goodwill	8,000	–	8,000	Balances b/d	33,000	12,000	30,000
Bank		16,000		Goodwill	8,000	4,000	4,000
Balances c/d	33,000	–	26,000				
	41,000	16,000	34,000		41,000	16,000	34,000
				Balances b/d	33,000	–	26,000

Task 2 **REENA AND TAMARA IN PARTNERSHIP**
STATEMENT OF FINANCIAL POSITION as at 1 September 20-8

	£
Non-current assets	50,000
Current assets	10,000
Cash and cash equivalents (£25,000 – £16,000)	9,000
	69,000
Trade payables	(10,000)
	59,000
Capital accounts	
Reena	33,000
Tamara	26,000
	59,000

7.4   **Task 1**

Date	Details	Reference	Dr	Cr
			£	£
20-8 1 Oct	Goodwill	GL	45,000	
	Capital – Dave	GL		22,500
	Capital – Elsa	GL		22,500
			45,000	45,000
	Goodwill created for the change in the profit-sharing ratio; credited to capital accounts in the partners' old profit-sharing ratio of 1:1			
1 Oct	Capital – Dave	GL	30,000	
	Capital – Elsa	GL	15,000	
	Goodwill	GL		45,000
			45,000	45,000
	Goodwill written off for the change in the profit-sharing ratio; debited to capital accounts in the partners' new profit-sharing ratio of 2:1			

Task 2

Dr   **Partners' capital accounts**   Cr

		Dave	Elsa			Dave	Elsa
20-8		£	£	20-8		£	£
1 Oct	Goodwill	30,000	15,000	1 Oct	Balances b/d	80,000	50,000
1 Oct	Balances c/d	72,500	57,500	1 Oct	Goodwill	22,500	22,500
		102,500	72,500			102,500	72,500
				1 Oct	Balances b/d	72,500	57,500

Task 3

DAVE AND ELSA IN PARTNERSHIP
STATEMENT OF FINANCIAL POSITION as at 1 October 20-8

	£
Net assets	130,000
Capital accounts:	
Dave	72,500
Elsa	57,500
	130,000

7.5   Task 1

JEAN AND DAVID
PARTNERSHIP APPROPRIATION ACCOUNT for the year ended 31 December 20-1

	Total	Jean	David
	£	£	£
Profit for the year	32,700		
Salaries	(22,000)	14,000	8,000
Interest on capital	(1,100)	500	600
Profit available for distribution	9,600		
Profit share:			
Jean	4,800		
David	4,800		
Total profit distributed	9,600		

Task 2

Dr				Partners' current accounts				Cr
		Jean	David				Jean	David
20-1		£	£	20-1			£	£
1 Jan	Balance b/d	–	1,250	1 Jan	Balance b/d		2,400	–
31 Dec	Drawings	18,600	14,200	31 Dec	Salaries		14,000	8,000
31 Dec	Balance c/d	3,100	–	31 Dec	Interest on capital		500	600
				31 Dec	Profit share		4,800	4,800
				31 Dec	Balance c/d		–	2,050
		21,700	15,450				21,700	15,450
20-2				20-2				
1 Jan	Balance b/d	–	2,050	1 Jan	Balance b/d		3,100	–

7.6   (a)   Capital account – Mel

Goodwill	4,800	Balance b/d	0
Balance c/d	25,200	Bank	30,000
	30,000		30,000

(b)   Goodwill can be defined as the difference between **the value of the business**, and the **net value** of the separate **assets and liabilities**.

CHAPTER 8: INTRODUCTION TO COMPANY FINANCIAL STATEMENTS

8.1 The main responsibilities of the directors of a limited company are to comply with the requirements of the Companies Act 2006 and with either International Financial Reporting Standards or Financial Reporting Standards. The directors must ensure that:

- the company keeps adequate accounting records sufficient to show and explain the company's transactions and to disclose the financial position

- financial statements are prepared at least annually (although some statements may cover periods of up to eighteen months)

- the annual financial statements are approved by the board of directors and signed, on behalf of the board, by a director whose signature must be on the statement of financial position

- a directors' report is prepared which includes a review of the activities of the company over the past year and of likely developments in the future

- the directors report annually to the company's shareholders on the way that they have run the company on behalf of the shareholders

- the annual financial statements and directors' report are filed with the Registrar of Companies where they are available for public inspection

8.2 **(a)** The statement of profit or loss of a limited company which meets the requirements of IAS 1 does not have to detail every single overhead or expense incurred. Instead, the main items are summarised, and a typical statement for a trading company – such as Beacon – will include the following:

- revenue
- cost of sales
- distribution costs
- administrative expenses
- finance costs
- tax expense

Further detail is usually provided to give information relevant to an understanding of financial performance.

The statement of profit or loss concludes by showing the profit or loss for the period attributable to equity holders.

(b) For the statement of profit or loss expenses must be analysed either:

- by nature (raw materials, employee costs, depreciation, etc), or
- by function (cost of sales, distribution costs, administrative expenses, etc)

The analysis selected will depend on which provides the more reliable and relevant information – the analysis by nature is often appropriate for manufacturing companies, while the analysis by function is commonly used by trading companies.

As Beacon Ltd is a trading company, the analysis by function would seem to be more appropriate.

8.3
- tax expense is shown as an expense in the statement of profit or loss
- property, plant and equipment is shown as a non-current asset in the statement of financial position
- finance costs are shown as an expense in the statement of profit or loss
- tax liabilities are shown as a current liability in the statement of financial position
- retained earnings is shown in the statement of changes in equity, and under the heading of issued capital and reserves in the statement of financial position

8.4 (a) IAS 1

8.5 (c) 1 and 3

Appendix:

photocopiable resources

These pages may be photocopied for student use, but remain the copyright of the author. It is recommended that they are enlarged to A4 size.

These pages are also available for download from the Resources Section of www.osbornebooks.co.uk

The forms and formats include:

Dr _____ account   Cr

Date	Details	Amount	Date	Details	Amount
		£			£

Dr _____ account   Cr

Date	Details	Amount	Date	Details	Amount
		£			£

Dr _____ account   Cr

Date	Details	Amount	Date	Details	Amount
		£			£

Dr _____ account   Cr

Date	Details	Amount	Date	Details	Amount
		£			£

STATEMENT OF PROFIT OR LOSS

of ....

for the year ended ....

	£	£
Sales revenue		
Cost of sales		
Gross profit		
Less expenses:		
Total expenses		
Profit for the year		

STATEMENT OF FINANCIAL POSITION

of ....

as at ....

	Cost £	Accumulated depreciation £	Carrying amount £
Non-current assets			
Current assets			
Current liabilities			
Net current assets			
Less Non-current liabilities			
Net assets			
Financed by:			Total £

Index

for your notes

for your notes